INFORMATION, IDEOLOGY AND COMMUNICATION

The New Nations' Perspectives on an Intellectual Revolution

Arnold Gibbons

UNIVERSITY
PRESS OF
AMERICA

LANHAM • NEW YORK • LONDON

For

My father and my mother

Maryse and Olivier

and

Juan Somavia

ACKNOWLEDGMENTS

Many people contributed to the writing of this
book. Donald P. Ely of Syracuse University encouraged
the original analysis and later on James Aronson read
portions of the manuscript and offered sound advice.
Aubrey Bonnett also of Hunter College was always concerned and offered suggestions from time to time. Jan
Plank of the University Press of America gave valuable
assistance.

Thanks to Doudou Diene, Director of the UNESCO
office at the United Nations, and to Soma Wijayadasa
and Anan Mahsuz, both of that organization, for their
assistance.

Mahdi Syad, the Somalian poet, was always ready to
render assistance even from a distance.

Maryse Kieffer-Gibbons encouraged an often recal-
citrant pen and to her I owe a debt of gratitude.
Virginia Aquino typed the manuscript.

TABLE OF CONTENTS

Table of Contents (<u>continued</u>)

PREFACE

Four main global trends marked the post World War II period. First, the growth of political ideology and the consequent hardening of attitudes, leading to confrontation between East and West. Second, the internationalization of social, economic and cultural affairs, which a world tormented by the horrors of war, believed necessary in order to survive; and from this feeling of common need, grew organizations such as the United Nations and its affiliated agencies, and also various alignments, notably the North Atlantic Treaty Organization. Third, the political independence of countries formerly subjugated by colonial power and the evolution of others to greater, if not limited participation in world affairs. Fourth, greater concern for poverty and welfare of countries which were poor and the resulting goodwill to remedy and redress wrongs, tempered by a liberal dosage of national self-interest.

Parallel with these trends was the increase in research and development, stimulating advanced technology which, with its consummate ability to harness limited resources and manpower to greater productivity, benefitted those countries which were able to take advantage of early opportunities centuries ago.

In its modern aspect, one strand of the growth of technology can be seen in the information industry. For example, in the U.S., "...Commerce Department reported results of its study that over 70 per cent of the U.S. work force is now employed within an information-based service sector, making a contribution of 65 per cent to the GNP, and approximately 25 per cent of total U.S. exports." 1/

The transistor revolutionized the communications industry. But what can be said for the computer?

1/ Eger, J. "Information, Informatics and International Information Flows: Predicates for New World Law and Policy". Address delivered at the Annenberg Conference on World Communications: Decisions for the Eighties, May 12-14, 1980.

While it has simplified things at one level, it has complicated them at another. Advanced computer technology now is the sacred preserve of rich countries and reflects the disturbing gap in riches, technology and information resources at all levels.

While these dizzying achievements in information technology take place, between the rich and the poor, discontent grows. Efforts are made to change the institutional structures at international organizations such as UNESCO. Information is seen increasingly as a commodity which benefits the rich to the detriment of the poor. A lack of understanding compounds the conflict. Issues divide the parties. Principles based on freedom of the press fill the air and the debate becomes bitter. No less than the harmony of international affairs is involved. And that harmony is temporarily shattered.

But it is clear that there is something else involved: another principle, perhaps unuttered: that is, the rich are never going to give up or surrender their riches. But despite the noise of the battle over the principle of freedom and the riches of resource is the need for understanding. It might well be that the controversy over information might have contributed to the beginning of a deeper understanding of the differences which distress the world. Such is my hope and that which informs this book.

INTRODUCTION

Information and communications technology have a profound effect on the course of modern events. This is not limited to the countries which are rich in information technology but also those which are poor in that area. Indeed, this book focuses on the relations between the rich and the poor countries which have come about as a result of this enormous gap in information technology.

These relations have affected both the domestic and international arenas. The earliest concerns were those echoed by those countries which emerged from the colonial era. These saw how communication channels supported and upkept colonial empires. As their own domestic and national policies were planned, they saw the need for improved information and communication structures. Internationally, they noticed the flow of information was unbalanced and controlled by a few countries. The one-way flow became their especial concern. It was through these means that the mass media of the advanced industrial countries was taking over their societies, and their institutions and making the task of development difficult. The cry was for an evaluation of this trend which almost seemed irreversible.

Deliberations were centered in two fora: the Non-Aligned Nations Tribunals and UNESCO. The non-aligned nations body was sympathetic. It was the appropriate forum for ventilating grievances of the developing countries which subscribed to the broad premise of the non-aligned philosophy. Numerous conferences were held in the decades of the sixties and seventies. Questions provoked by the one-way flow of information and the attendant influences of information and technology in general—such as the increasing power of transnational corporations—became the focus of attention. Resolutions were passed condemning what was considered to be exploitative practices.

UNESCO, the other body, also came in for much attention; and the developing countries perceived the organization as a final hope for the airing of their grievances. Freedom of the press was an important issue raised by these countries. They consider it as a vestige of the supremacy of the rich countries which would use this as a means of supporting and propping up their supremacy. The freedom of the press is not held with the same importance.

The decade of the seventies marked conspicuous attempts to revise the information and technology biases, as they were considered by the poor countries. The dialogue covered other areas as well. It became part of the on-going and bitter conflict between the so-called countries to the North and countries to the South. UNESCO became the battlefield of attempts to institutionalize changes which were and are considered important for the welfare of the poor countries.

The 'Right to communicate' became part of the general discourse. This involved the right of individuals as well as governments to participate in the field of information. Access and participation were the common goals to be shared by mankind. And a redress of the imbalance in information and communication became the sought-after objective at UNESCO.

It is against this background that one understands the move towards politicization of the information fields, with the developing countries on the one hand and the developed countries on the other, and the other gaps which exist between them, created and extended by the new technologies.

It is clear from the continuing debate that the rich countries are not about to surrender their gains or lead in the information and communication fields, though it is increasingly evident that they realize that they must share. They must share because the solution to world problems demand common goals and a wider vision.

Chapter 1

THE EMERGING DEBATE

Widespread growth in communications technology
has extended the frontiers of knowledge and trans-
formed the environment in which we live. Each country
now reflects in some form, the sophistication of
modern communications technology, which involves the
individual and society in a more dynamic way than it
ever did before. The combination of men and machines
now touches the lives of all people, bringing about
conspicuous change not only in their daily lives, but
also in their environment. In the U.S. this can be
seen in the influence of television on politics, human
behavior and the lives of children. Internationally,
it is observed in the application of organizational
and management sciences to international affairs,
business, trade and industry. Also, there is evidence
of the increasing importance of transnational corporations in computer communications and transborder data
flow.

While the hardware of the communications process
might be the same, the application of it and the way
it is used differs from country to country. Culture
and how it is organized influence influences the way a
country handles its messages and the content of its
messages. Indeed, the communication explosion has
three distinct characteristics: geographical, in the
sense that it is worldwide and encompasses most countries in some form or other, and no country is free
from its influence; the proliferation of various messages; and its technical capacity, which is to say,
the tendency for equipment to proliferate as a consequence of mass production of goods.

There is a close connection between these three
characteristics which, among others, such as language,
culture and population, persuade the communications
process. Most of the startling advances in technology
have taken place in Europe and America and these have,
in turn, affected the enormous amount of messages,
which are put out daily from newspapers, television
and radio stations and the business world via the computer. Inventions in scientific technology have
brought about swift changes in the hardware of communications. For example, advances in microphotography

1

have made it possible to record printed material on a microfiche card, thus minimizing problems of storage and space. Also, the high standard of literacy in Europe and America has encouraged greater participation in national development as well as stimulated interest in individual and personal development.

In addition, economic progress has both reinforced and been reinforced by improvements in technology. Rich countries can afford advanced communication systems, whereas it is only with difficulty that poor countries can, if at all, manage to keep up in the race. Indeed, poor countries are unable to fully participate either in their own national economic development, because of insufficient funds, or, because they lack the necessary information strategy to promote national development. These countries are handicapped because they do not have telecommunication facilities, which could enable them to take _immediate_ advantage of better facilities. Finally, as the poor countries lie predominantly in the tropic zone, communication is often unreliable because of ionospheric conditions brought about by the sun.

Differences in language also create problems. In many countries a profusion of native languages prevent adequate communication and interpersonal relations must be conducted in the language spoken by the elite, which usually is in the minority. 1/ For example, the government of the Ivory Coast, keenly aware of the perplexity among its 60 different language groups, instituted French as the lingua franca and the largest instructional project in the world is involved in language training. In the U.S., relative language homogeneity has prevented this problem from occurring, though in New York City, the Hispanic population has undermined the claims of English to exclusivity. But the limitations of language do not greatly affect the world expansion of communication facilities, though they do affect communication within a given country. What promoted increased interest and involvement in international news and its distribution was world conflict: World War II led to the expansion of news agencies.

International news and agencies

Global conflict initiated an era of international concern, not least because so many countries were

2

involved. This continued after World War II ended, with the creation of international and other quasi-regulatory agencies.

Four main tendencies marked this period. First, the growth of political ideology and the hardening of attitudes, which led to confrontation between East and West. Second, the internationalization of social, economic and cultural affairs, which a world tormented by the horrors of war, believed necessary in order to survive; and from this feeling of common need, grew such organizations like the United Nations and its affiliated agencies, and various alignments such as the North Atlantic Treaty Organization. Third, the political independence of countries formerly subjugated by colonial power; and the evolution of others to greater, if not limited participation in world affairs. Fourth, greater concern for poverty and welfare of countries that were poor and the resulting goodwill to remedy and redress wrongs, tempered by a liberal dosage of national self-interest.

Despite many protestations on the part of wealthy countries, this continues to be a sore point with the poor, who complain bitterly that the aid of the wealth is "honored more in the breach than in the observance" and that despite the rhetoric, exploitation still is rampant. 2/

In fact, the final consequence of World War II was the widening of the gap between the rich and the poor. This is partly due to increase in research and development and the rise of modern technology. Technology, with its consummate ability to harness limited resources and manpower to greater productivity, brought wealth to those countries which were able to take advantage of opportunities for expansion centuries ago. 3/

In its modern idiom the growth of technology can be seen in the information industry. For example, the transitor revolutionized the electronic industry and brought a distant world closer to millions. The electronic computer increased storage, retrieval and organizational capacities of enormous amounts of information. While the transistor is within reach of the masses in the developing world, complicated computer systems are beyond their availability. Cable has opened up two-way communication between household and information services and attached to a computer

3

can handle information beyond the capacity of the telephone. 4/ Telephone services for the household expand to include the picturephone, a visual screen attached to the telephone. A bewildering array of services and developments flows from computer technology,
resulting in the transmission of information from
centers such as libraries, supermarkets, shopping
plazas to the home. Apart from information for consumer interest, it is anticipated that news services
will be assembled and compiled with an eye to greater
specialization of copy and shown on home video screens.

News and wire services now placed on the computer
in digital form, facilitate recall and further communication with other sources of information and distribution. Technological developments in the news field
are revolutionizing news gathering as well as the dissemination process. Information becomes available
sooner and quicker to the consumer and international
events are as immediate as the accident on Main Street.
An informed public has the wherewithal for participation in world affairs. But this advanced technology
is at the moment only available in the rich industrial
countries.

The introduction of news technology changes social
behavior. 5/ Information, once the sacred, guarded
prerogative of the affluent, becomes the property of
Everyman and, stripped of its mystery, is shared by all.
Messages freely circulate a system, limited only by the
availability of the channels and ability of the receiver to interpret. Dependence on information, which
created social hierarchy, breaks down and those people
who now find themselves exposed to information channels actively use them. The transistor in certain regions of Africa enabled schemes of social development,
including health, welfare and farming projects to be
launched. The new technology also permanently altered
social relations, opening wider national debate and
encouraging participation in national and international affairs.

Press and broadcasting: ethical
considerations

Increased channels of communication help citizens
to monitor the work of government and other agencies.
With more information available through increased news
circulation, the response from pressure groups and
citizen lobbies to national and international issues

4

becomes more active. Criticism of government is
healthy at the best of times and essential for the
health of the body politic. On the other hand, criticism of government is frowned on in certain systems
of government that limit popular influence on national affairs and minimize input in the formulation of
social policy. More channels of communication accel-
erate relations among a broad range of social groups,
nourish and foster a wide canvas of opinion and points
of view. The inevitable consequence of differing
political philosophies is a difference in attitude to
the news process, the practice of journalism, and also
relations between countries. It is the battleground
of the struggle between the countries that make up the
Third World and essentially the rich countries of the
West, though others are not excluded.

The Third World refers to those countries which
feel themselves victimized by poverty, malnutrition,
underdevelopment and powerlessness and these amount to
at least half the world's people. The Third World has
grown out of particular experience; its press systems
therefore reflect it and must be understood as a corrective to it.

According to Pierre Julee, 6/ the expression was
first used in 1956, referring to those countries which
fell neither under the capitalist nor the socialist
umbrella, but rather into a formal class of their own.
However, since there are few such countries, if any,
the expression seems inaccurate and misplaced. In
fact, most Third World countries fall squarely into
one camp or other, thus underlining their special relationship to both systems, and this accounts for a
great deal of the confusion. Hence the Third World
is not a separate entity, which its title seems to
imply. But where meaning is confusing, usage is not,
and the Third World is a familiar expression if not a
household term.

Because of the growth, strength, and absorptive
capacity of rich countries, these Third World countries wage an ever increasing battle for economic survival. In a world dominated by power relations--
both Western and Eastern--they have found it necessary to defend their growing, fledgling systems by
various means. The institutions of the press are only
one means. The conflict between newly independent
countries and others is not only about the plight of
the past. It has to do with the reality of the

5

present and the concerns of the day as reflected in the news. Race is an ever present state of affairs.

The news is that there is a constant and continuing attempt by white people to influence, if not control, the lives and policies of non-white people. This is one meaning of power. But this is not only a condition of political influence; it can be seen more clearly in economic matters. It is the studied attempt "to prevent newly independent nations from consolidating their independence and thus to keep them economically dependent and securely in the world capitalist system." 7/

The institutions of the Third World are also influenced by such social ingredients as slavery, ethnic stratification, social class systems and racism--all appendages of colonialism. A failure to understand the effect of these influences hinders understanding of the current attitude of the press in the Third World.

Their press systems contend on two fronts: first, economic and social development; and second, political independence. The press is often the only form of defense available to some of these countries. To the Western world, a lack of press freedom is often seen as an incursion on individual freedom. This must be despised in the extreme, or at least patronized, when it falls short of libertarian standards.

The Third World, however, regards its press as a necessary weapon to combat fearsome odds that seek to conquer it, and a necessary defense against aggression in whatever guise it may come. This combativeness is not simply directed at the enemy without, but more especially, at the enemy within, for neo-colonial institutions still persist; and their supporters undermine national loyalty by encouraging unnecessary dissent.

Dissent is not just opposition to a Bill under consideration in the National Assembly to be dealt with in routine debate. It is more than that. Dissent assumes a seriousness which to Western eyes seems out of proportion to its value. This is because we are dealing with countries, in which choice is severely limited and alternatives few. The choice may be at times a painful one, for it concerns life or death. The choice may be not whether to import guns or butter, but whether to import at all, because to import is to drain limited foreign currency and deplete reserves. When survival is at stake, debate can be a luxury, except where it is likely to clarify the issues.

But although the choice may be at times cruel, these countries have approached the problem in different ways. It is an error to consider the Third World as a monolith, sharing the same problems and the same fate. Its members share very different political ideologies, ranging from the Marxism of Angola, Mozambique, Zimbabwe, Cuba to the capitalism of Trinidad and Tobago and the Ivory Coast. Their governments also are assorted and include parliamentary democracies as well as dictatorships and an indescribable melange of administrative and representative convenience. Also, some are run by the military. They have various and varying levels of development, from the more advanced oil states of Saudi Arabia and Kuwait, to less advanced Tanzania and Ethiopia. But their interests tend to be the same when faced by the dominant world of the West. Despite differences in ideology, government and economic development, they display a remarkable ability to close ranks when they feel threatened. And each country responds to a perceived threat in a way that is appropriate and in keeping with its own vision of itself and its future. Problems of survival also influence decisions and many of these problems predate political independence, or are a consequence of it.

Political independence, which was achieved by many in the 1960s, stimulated discussions about institutions in general and their relationship to them in particular. One such concept is freedom, which came under consistent and close scrutiny. Indeed, the examination of freedom and its implications sheds new light on a concept, which has been much taken for granted: the freedom of the press.

Much controversy and discussion surround the freedom and responsibility of the press. The rush for modernization and the corresponding demands on the social, economic and political institutions of young countries, brought about a conflict between traditional and modern practices. Governments committed to national development are not likely to be over concerned with the rights and liberties of the individual, whom they see as obstacles in the development process. The institution of the press is one such obstacle.

7

The press traditionally has been a sacred cow in Western countries. After the initial period of doubt and confusion surrounding its establishment in the seventeenth century, the press has persisted to this day as an indispensable component in the working life of the citizens of the State; and if its influence has at times been overpowering, if not overbearing, it has at least the considerable virtue of keeping a wary eye and watchful on governments. The press is a necessary ingredient in the working life of the State, to be questioned, examined, criticized, but never to be dispensed with.

Western scholars have on the whole been intoxicated by the concept of the freedom of the press and have dismissed as nonvirtuous any departures from this standard, defined less by the realism of that standard than by an absolute philosophical premise.

Until recently, there has been no compelling need to discuss the Third World and press freedom and their problems have been looked on as their own particular concerns, of casual importance to the rest of the world. Now that we are all faced with common problems in the midst of shrinking world resources, it has become fashionable to treat these countries more seriously. Also, a self-righteousness about the sacredness of press freedom has excluded any other considerations.

This is a pity, for so much has changed and is changing in the twentieth century, and not least of all in the very liberal philosophy, of which the free press is a part. And there is science and an expanding technology to influence social change and the way we look at ourselves. Third World countries mirror these concerns. In many instances they share like Caliban a common heritage with former colonial masters and like Caliban can now say:

You taught me language and the profit on't
Is that I know how to curse...

Much has been written elsewhere about this relationship between former colonial power and independent country. 8/ 9/ The psychological aspect of this relationship underlines much of the current aggravation over the free press. These countries refuse to pay lip service to what they consider as abstract principle, declining to honor in theory a concept which is not fully realizable in practice. They voice the view

8

that the problems of national development do not allow
such luxuries.

Indeed, national development and the theories
upon which it is based, exemplifies the difference
between Third World countries and most Western theories of development. 10/ 11/ 12/ These theories
generally see the development process as one of enlightenment, e.g., when an individual becomes more informed and knowledgeable, he will want to participate
more fully in national development. Common to these
theories is their ethnocentrism and identification of
Western life styles with the needs of Third World countries. The presumption here is that the exposure of
people to the good life motivates them to bring changes
in their own; follows then the desire to accumulate
material goods and their values.

Finally, there is the view, shared by the more
technologically sophisticated countries of the East,
that Third World countries are a tabula rasa, waiting
on external stimulus to nudge them into the modern
world. This does not square with the facts. 13/ Much
of this jaundiced thinking has affected the mass media
of communication, which are seen as obvious and indis-
putable channels for information and education. But
the mass media, and more especially, the press, in
their propaganda and public opinion functions merit
study.

Propaganda and public opinion

The functions of propaganda and public opinion
are undergoing change. Public opinion is not the cul-
mination of reasoned debate, (if it ever was) when
contrasting and often conflicting ideas are discussed
and threshed out in public forum or private caucus,
the end result of which is an informed public and a
knowledgeable citizen. Propaganda has replaced public
opinion and the contest is not over ideas, but the
conquest of the individual psyche. McLuhan has suggested that the speed at which information flows
through the electronic media has prevented rational
decision-making, which may be true. The television
audience is on the whole passive, as a consequence of
which propaganda is much more easily accepted as programming. Television has affected people's perception
of the print medium and also the institutions of the
print medium.

9

In Third World countries, press freedom has been challenged, deliberately in some cases, and more subtly in others. The expansion of technology in the twentieth century has been accompanied by social dislocation and the collapse of those institutions not strong enough to withstand its pressures. Recent administrative institutions, such as government bureaucracies and the national press, are unable generally to oppose these pressures successfully. Those which possess some flexibility survive; others less flexible succumb. The influx of technology has been sometimes accompanied by the displacement of the individual, bombarded by a plethora of competing loyalties. These create havoc, uncertainty and chaos; they assault values loosely held and destroy them. One of the results of information dissemination has been the involvement by a majority of the citizens in widespread abuses. There can no longer be an uninvolved citizen.

Propaganda has replaced debate as the public philosophy and idols of the market place have now become quantitative rather than qualitative. Words such as growth, saturation, increase, loss, ratings, indices, now underline the new public understanding. Dialogue, which used to be an offshoot of liberalism, has also changed to match the new spirit of the times. Public interest in affairs is evidenced by exchange rather than discussion and dialogue. This curtails individual choice, for people cannot choose unless they have information on which to base that choice. All governments to some degree restrict choice--on security grounds, for example. Propaganda, which is the establishment's or government's answer to real or imagined threats from outside, is now an active force within the government apparatus, active and devoted to the subjugation of individual psyche. On the international level it is the battle between conflicting ideologies: communism and capitalism. It is a contest to determine preferences. The very media used to promote debate stifles it by insisting on participating in the debate, thus directing and, perhaps, controlling it. This is an example of what Ellul calls integration propaganda, which is the social adjustment of society by means of the media to the rules of the governing establishment. 14/

Third World countries have within their societies the preconditions for rebellion and revolution. In some the discarding of the colonial power was itself a

10

revolutionary act and the maintenance of revolutionary fervor is a requirement for national development. Developing institutions, which cannot cope with the information explosion because of inadequate resources and skilled personnel, are often in conflict with a governing elite anxious to get on with the work of development. The elite finds it easier to govern by fiat and authority. The clash of the new technology and old tradition holds for an uneasy peace. Western self-righteousness, occasional ridicule and external criticism, create a climate of defiance and arrogance within. Criticism from within is interpreted as a sell-out to the enemy--variously referred to as imperialist-- and therefore to be silenced. Finally, ideology, a fashionable attribute of modern societies, requires an alignment of forces on the road to a presumed Utopia. Propaganda joins forces with capitalism or communism, with a free press or with a controlled press.

Press freedom defined

The concept of the freedom of the press is often treated by the Western press as an either/or proposition. Either the press is free or it is not free. This is simplistic and a viewpoint, which does not contribute to the continuing debate about the quality of institutions, or to the philosophical foundations of liberalism in an era of change. It is precisely because of this that debate must continue.

In the West, a denial of press freedom indicates a betrayal of principle, which, to dismiss, suggests intolerance and insensitivity. It is to condemn without hearing and to judge without knowledge. The fact is that Third World countries are heirs to two contrasting traditions of the press: the libertarian and the totalitarian. The former is grounded in the philosophical tradition of Mills and eighteenth century rationalism and the turbulent history of press freedom in the seventeenth and nineteenth centuries. Totalitarianism has come to be identified with Marx, though it does not derive from Marx.

Lenin considered the press as a scientific component of a scientific society. The press as an arm of the State had a certain prescribed role. Third world countries, torn between the two contrasting philosophies, both ideologically and operationally, find neither completely adequate for their purposes.

11

Traditional press freedom rules out decisive
government influence, runs the argument against a completely free press. But they ask how can the press
succeed in its mission without government influence?
In many cases, government is the largest single employer in the State, and some of its members were key
figures in the independence struggle. Rely on the
overseas press? The answer is obvious. No independent country of the kind under consideration can long
allow the voice of foreign interests to speak for it,
from within or without. Recent history suggests mis-
representation and sensationalism; furthermore, how
can countries like the U.S. and Britain, to mention but
two, which have had difficulty reporting their own
minorities do any better in overseas countries?

Third World countries cannot allow foreign news
agencies to dominate the reporting of news because of
a presumed hostility, which practice occasionally sub-
stantiates. A free press, in the opinion of these
countries, can only survive in an atmosphere of trust,
mutual trust. Finally, the argument concludes: government participation in the press is necessary to influence, cajole, impress and stimulate the development
process.

The case against the communist press is equally
powerful, in their view. While on the one hand the
communist press ensures total government control of all
communications, it does not allow citizens to actively
participate in policy at a meaningful level. In addition, the communist press does not seem able to provide a _flexible_ format for political and economic
development beyond Marxist ideology. The communist
press in general is rigid without being benevolent and
unable to avoid the threats to individual freedom,
which sometimes follows the absence of institutional
freedom.

Neither the libertarian nor the communist tradition seems to have safeguards or the elasticity which
the Third World in general is prepared to accept.
While libertarianism entails press freedom, it is at
the expense--as the Third World sees it--of government
participation; and it wishes government to participate
in the role of the press. The communist press does
not safeguard the rights of citizens and may undermine
the development process. Needed is a system that
honors the government's right to discharge its obligations, as it sees them, and the citizen's right to

12

speak without fear. This is idealistic. But it is
precisely what the question is all about. Third World
countries need an idealism to face the hard reality of
their problems.

Idealism and its implications

Indeed, the problems of national development,
among others such as perception of their position in
the international arena, increasing political influence,
global political awareness, have led the Third World
to challenge the fundamental bases of international
communication. Information can flow freely in the absence of impediment and if there are sufficient channels of communication; correspondingly, a lack of
available channels restricts flow. Hence the free
flow of information is meaningful only to those countries that have the channels and without substance to
those that do not. Again, information is closely related to economic hegemony and the extension of power
and influence; and those countries, which have ample
means of communication, use information as a means to
further national, economic and political objectives.

There is a greater flow of information from rich
countries to poor countries, from countries of the
North to countries to the South. This is not accidental: information channels followed old colonial
routes, and with this traffic utilization, a continuation of colonial patterns of economic and cultural
domination. 15/ If colonial empires were said to have
been acquired in a fit of absentmindedness, the enormous economic and cultural expansion of the industrial
powers following World War II, was a result of deliberate policy. 16/ What had been true of the active
period of colonial expansion, when supposedly flag
followed trade, is equally true in mid-twentieth century: trade follows communication channels.

The Third World believes that in matters of trade
they are substantially second class citizens, unable
to control the marketing of their raw materials and to
demand fair prices for them. Hence, the relationship
between the doctrine of the free flow of information
and economic dependency becomes apparent. Unable then
to reverse the free flow of information--in reality, a
one-way flow--and to gain access to industrial markets
on conditions of parity, leads to increasing frustration and consequent demands for a change in the status
quo. The idea of a free and balanced flow of

information between countries must be seen as a response to an unbalanced flow of information, which perpetuates inequality among countries.

Increased access to channels of communication, multi-way information flow and enhanced participation among countries deprived of both channels and rights of access, is the case upon which the Third World rests its claims. These claims are a challenge to the entire system of international communication. What is being challenged is no less than the pulse of the international communication system that has defined relations between countries and is the basis of Article 19 of the Universal Declaration of Human Rights. 17/

> "Everyone has the right to freedom of opinion and expression; this right included freedom to hold opinions without interference and to seek, receive and impart information and ideas through any media and regardless of frontiers."

But clearly "the right ...to seek, receive and impart information" is a qualified and not an absolute right. Access to the media for everyone, which may have nothing to do with access at all, but on finance, race, political power and public relations dexterity and so on. Furthermore, the framers of the Universal Declaration and its thirty articles were limited to considering the print medium and did not envisage the extensive technology that was later to follow.

Technological developments impose greater strain on the Universal Declaration of Human Rights doctrine, making demands on it, which the original architects did not at the time foresee. For example, the Human Rights doctrine cannot be universalized; second, it does not carry the force of law but of moral sanction; and third, it does not discriminate between the social right to seek, receive and impart information and the individual right to seek, receive and impart information. This last point is crucial, for it seeks to expand the doctrine to both the individual as well as to society. Finally, the right to seek, receive and impart information is a function of technological processes--satellites, cable systems, news agencies, information and data based systems etc.--as well as sources of information, and international power. In these areas the Third World countries are inadequate.

The inadequacy of this doctrine for Third World needs is thrown into sharp relief by its exercise in practice. The free flow of information principle enshrined in the Universal Declaration of Human Rights, becomes in the hands of Western powers, an instrument for the perpetuation of narrow self-interests and the propagation of these interests to the exclusion of other possibilities. It becomes identified with the furtherance of economic and political interests and of peripheral concern to the full and wider implications of the doctrine. Freedom of information becomes the euphemism for trade and commercial expansion of Western powers, basking in technological mastery, while international organizations provide a moral umbrella for their actions. They care less about countries that have not yet defined a policy to shelter their inadequacy.

If freedom consists in the ability to "seek alternative possibilities", then it is a contradiction to deny this right to groups such as governments. The Western idea of freedom is centered in the individual, even though in practice this freedom is exercised by groups, e.g., transnational corporations, press conglomerates, television networks, to name a few. Freedom is the exercise of the group acting on behalf of the individual. Some Third World countries want their governments to exercise a more balanced flow of information. They claim there is no contradiction here, as long as freedom is not denied the individual in their societies.

But to maintain a plausible philosophical position means nothing in the face of impotence in the international field, which is already the exclusive property of Western powers and in particular the U.S. 18/

The Third World quickly came to realize, as their countries set about the task of formulating national policy, that they cannot separate social, economic, cultural and political policies into watertight compartments, for the assault from the West and also the East --though the quality and the quantity of the latter's influence is no match for the energy of the former--is total. Public as well as private interests pursue divergent as well as convergent claims through social, cultural and political policies. 19/ Countries that had hitherto treated cultural traffic as an innocent if pleasant diversion, became aware that innocence can be deceptive. They see an economic invasion supported

15

by a comprehensive cultural policy in the process of diluting their nationalism.

Free and balanced flow

Cultural imperialism and its apparent evils are the sign of the new awareness. The unmasking of the motives of the industrial conglomerate, led to attempts on the international field for a "free and balanced" flow of information. UNESCO, which had been in the vanguard of the free flow movement, fittingly now leads the attempts to consider the full implications of it, how inequitably it is applied.

It was at a meeting of UNESCO's experts in Montreal in June 1969 that the one way flow of information and the unbalanced flow of information were first considered and entered the vocabulary of modern communications. The free and balanced flow concept was derived, together with matters peripheral to the communications field, such as resources, media channels, satellites and communication rights. News agencies were identified as the subjects of cultural imperialism. Several writers pointed to the disquieting fact that a small number of news agencies are responsible for a disproportionate say in the world and peddle an enormous influence. That these news agencies "belong to" countries of importance is by no means coincidental. Corporate power and national hegemony are bedfellows.

The four Western news agencies: Associated Press (AP), United Press International (UPI), Reuters, and Agence France Presse (AFP) are prestigious organizations, gathering, selling and distributing news on all five continents, and in the view of the Third World, monopolizing the news business. Because of their combined influence, continue the complaints, the news agencies are in a position to define what news is all about and to bring their own ethnocentric view to the definition. Because of which, they pay scant attention to what is newsworthy than to what is sensational. Disasters, catastrophes and natural hazards and events of like nature, which titillate the fancy of the home audience become grist for the mill.

The Third World complains that insensitivity to its concerns is evidence of the stanglehold on international news by the news agencies and their countries of origin. It is part of the general policy of the

16

West, which includes among other elements: advertising, television, computer technology and data banks.

The association of news agencies and countries of origin, do not complete the picture however. The multinational corporation also spreads its giant tentacles, reaching out to whatever is profitable and supporting with influence, capital and technical expertise, the continuation of economic subjugation if not servitude. The close ties between economics and information control are further strengthened in the view of these countries by the harsh reality of development problems. Needing money for development, "development aid", they must borrow at exorbitant rates of interest from the very countries which maintain this economic strangulation and monopoly of news and information systems. These are the very countries which support a free and unfettered information flow. Moreover, they complain that Western-owned banks such as the International Bank for Reconstruction and Development (The World Bank) are not always sensitive to their problems. 20/

The Third World believes that there is a "conspiracy" among Western countries to dictate by means of the collusion of government and private interests represented by the giant transnational corporations. This "conspiracy" also includes the denigration of national culture by overexposure to alien cultural artifacts. And it further includes the influence of domestic and foreign policy by the release of only such information that is in keeping with stereotypic images. Thus, economic realities, political ideology, national self-interest and culture are directly related to the free flow of information. It is not surprising therefore that the Right to Communicate became part of the public agenda and with it consideration of a New World Information Order.

The right to communicate

This is the current response to the frustration of the Third World and other countries at the present unbalanced free flow of information system, which appears to be in the interests of rich and powerful countries. The right to communicate seeks to explore new avenues for the communication of information in a way which would be more equitable. Four aspects are considered. 21/

The first seeks to examine the philosophical premise upon which communication rests within the framework of the Universal Declaration of Human Rights. The second identifies specific areas which are applicable to human and national communication needs: the Outer Space Treaty and the Copyright Law are examples. The third and fourth aspects taken together are the foci of Third World concerns. Both relate to problems of economic, social, cultural and political questions. Also, the attendant question as to what is to be done to the environment so that it reflects wider national and international participation and a more equitable disposition of the world's resources.

The importance of a fair solution to the problems of information overload and scarcity, cannot be overemphasized. The right to communicate, as it applies to rich and poor countries and the North and South dialogue envisages access and participation and continuing dialogue at all levels. 22/

Implicit in this statement by Gunnar Naesselund, Director of UNESCO's Department of Free Flow of Information and Development of Communication, is a view of world communications in which both governments and private individuals and groups have the same right. It is an extension of the free flow of information principle, which had been the mainstay of national and international communication in the years after World War II, and in which the Third World, for reasons already outlined, remained excluded.

It is for this reason that the Third World places so much importance on the New World Information Order. The right to communicate is the premise on which the New World Information Order can be based, in much the same way as the free flow of information was the foundation of the old order, which is associated with inequity and imbalance. The right to communicate concept encourages the optimism that a two-way flow of information would replace a one-way flow, which created monopoly and dependence.

Many say the concept is vague and meaningless. Others can see no reason for changing the basis for international communication. They point to Article 19 of the Universal Declaration of Human Rights as a firm foundation for international communication.

Meanwhile, concurrent with this debate, the argument over the New World Information Order gains momentum and is at center stage. The Third World is determined that its interests, which it identifies with both this Order as well as the New International Economic Order, will not be set aside. But the forces arraigned against it and the power brokers may just be too powerful to allow international sanction to interests, which seem to oppose the status quo.

Nonetheless, the writer sets out to explore the relationship between the old order and the new emerging one. Also, certain aspects of this relationship, lost in the clatter and traffic of contemporary debate, will be considered.

A work of this kind, which seeks to understand and to explain, must inevitably be descriptive and discursive. It is well to remember that Third World countries are undergoing change, developing and encouraging their institutions to establish priorities and to find ways of achieving goals. But the rich countries and those who for varying reasons feel threatened by <u>all</u> Third World movements, are also undergoing change, and often, in spite of themselves, as a <u>result</u> of changes in the Third World. Change is, therefore, for most countries, an on-going condition, a continuing exercise. Debate about information and economics is therefore as incomplete as the development process itself. And the time is ripe for broader and more meaningful participation in international affairs. One way to reflect this is an understanding of the issues.

Notes

1/ Gibbons, A. "French West Africa." In Sydney W. Head (ed.), Broadcasting in Africa. Philadelphia: Temple University Press, 1975.

2/ Jalee, P. Pillage of the Third World. New York: Monthly Review Press, 1968.

3/ Bagdikian, B. The Information Machines. New York: Random House, 1974.

4/ Bagdikian, B. Op. cit., 1974.

5/ Innis, H. Bias in Communications. Toronto: University of Toronto Press, 1964.

6/ Jalee, P. Op. cit., 1968.

7/ Fann, K. T. & Hodges, D. C. (ed.). Readings in U.S. Imperialism. Boston: Porter Sargent Publisher, 1971.

8/ Mannoni, O. Prospero and Caliban. London: Methuen, 1956.

9/ Fanon, F. The Wretched of the Earth. New York: Vikings Press, 1969.

10/ McClelland, D. The Achieving Society. Cambridge: Harvard University Press, 1962.

11/ Pool, I. de Sola. "The Mass Media and Politics in the Modernization Process." In L. Pye (ed.), Communications and Political Development. Princeton: Princeton University Press, 1963.

12/ Golding, P. "Media's Role in National Development," Journal of Communication, Summer 1974.

13/ Ellul, J. Propaganda: the Formation of Men's Attitudes. New York: Vintage Books, 1973.

14/ Cherry, C. Op. cit., 1971.

15/ Schiller, H. Instant Research on Peace and Violence. Finland: Tampere Research Institute, 1975.

16/   United Nations document. OPI/18574-150M.

17/   Tunstall, J. The Media are American. New York: Columbia University Press, 1977.

18/   Schiller, H. Mass Communications and American Empire. New York: Augustus M. Kelley, Publishers, 1969.

19/   Manley, M. Prime Minister of Jamaica. An Address at Hunter College, November 22, 1978.

20/   Harms, R., Richstad, J. & Kie, K. Right to Communicate. Honolulu: University of Hawaii, 1977.

21/   Naesselund, G. "Relations between and perspectives within development support communication, communication policy research and planning, and the right to communicate as seen by UNESCO." In Harms, Richstad and Kie, Right to Communicate. Honolulu: University of Hawaii, 1977.

Chapter 2

ISSUES AT STAKE

The main issues on the agenda of the Third World
are clear: the implications of what the freedom of
the press is really all about; media power; messages
from industrialized countries, which often offend
national sensitivities. The same issues can be sub-
divided into a host of other attributes, equally sensitive, equally important and equally troublesome.

They concern governments of countries to the East
and governments and countries to the West; world organizations such as the United Nations and UNESCO; the
major news agencies and the newspapers which provide
copy; radio and television networks, which have interests the world over; the transnational corporations,
which influence world economic policy; non-governmental
organizations such as Freedom House, which support a
free press; citizen lobbies; private foundations; and
also people from the academic world. Their confrontation already is a cause celebre.

The issues are philosophic, for press freedom is
a basic western concept central to liberty. But they
are also about power, the abuse of power, the lack of
it, for those countries which have power can and usually succeed in utilizing it whatever way they choose,
be it economic, cultural or political. And in practice
there is no distinction between economics, culture and
politics, for media power does not discriminate; and
evenhandedly, if not heavy handedly, the media dominate wherever they may. While the philosophical concerns are important because they affect the fundamental
premise of Western attitudes towards the press, they
are not the only consideration. The Soviet Union also
challenges the Western domination of the communications
media, for reasons quite apart from those of the Third
World and the West.

There is UNESCO, which acts as honest broker, trying to reconcile the legitimate interests of the Third
World with those of the industrial countries. It is an
uncomfortable role, for it lays itself open to attack
from all parties and raises questions as to whether
that organization should defend the policies of the
majority, or its most powerful representatives.

23

Also, the question, which has not been much aired, is the extent to which UNESCO should, given the expertise it draws on, lead a movement in which it believes, if it believes that movement to be in the interests of stability and world equilibrium; or, should it follow the dictates of member nations that comprise it. These questions are not academic, for they concern the vitality and credibility of an international organization set up to resolve disputes which affect harmony among nations.

Freedom of the press, media power and cultural imperialism emerge from an economic condition. That condition is one of economic development and the inequities of the world trading system which denies the Third World a fair share of markets and also fair prices for raw materials. The importance of economics and its connection with information is best understood by a historical appraisal of the world system since the end of World War II.

The defeat of Germany symbolized the end of an active period of colonial power (it is often forgotten that Germany was a colonial power, having colonies in East Africa). The fact that the end was brought about by other colonial powers does not detract from its significance. Germany's defeat was as much the defeat of oppression as the defeat of an idea--the notion of race and cultural supremacy based on social and economic growth. The clock could not therefore be put back to the status quo before World War II, a fact which Roosevelt realized and Churchill did not. It was somewhat of a contradiction to defeat an idea and to perpetuate the same idea in practice, a lesson learned readily enough by the future leaders of the then colonial countries, which participated in World War II. But the colonial system could not be brought to an end by the stroke of a pen. An institution, which had dominated the world for three centuries, could not willingly bring about its own demise, without attempting to salvage a piece from the wreckage. Only too well aware of the implications of the end of its own supremacy, colonial powers sought to honor the movement towards independence in theory, while devising means for continuing economic domination in practice.

Thus, this period is considered to be one of the watersheds of history, when the old order disguises itself and the same patterns of behavior reassert themselves in different form. What changed was the method of exploitation, which became more urbane and refined in order to deal with newly independent countries. Methods rather than policy changed.

It was relatively easy for this colonial traffic to maintain itself in economic ascendancy, while paying lip service to economic and political independence. First, the colonial trade ensured the maintenance of commerce and industry and the lines of communication assured its viability. Political independence did not change the sea routes between England and the West Indies, nor did it change the lines of communication between England and India, nor did relations between France and her former African colonies substantially change after independence. In fact, post-independence relations showed every indication of expanding, judging by the increased trading relations and bilateral trade agreements, which defined dealings between the metropolitan power and the former colonial territories.

The new countries were persuaded that these "arrangements" were in their favor. It was not terribly difficult to do this, for the euphoria of independence, added to token development needs which were never touched, usually brought in some cosmetic riches to the elite of their societies. Meanwhile, incomplete development projects continued like a distant mirage to beckon longingly from a distance, providing false hope, but destined never to leave the drawing board, if ever they reached that far.

This relationship was accompanied by limited economic gains for the new countries, as their emersion in the imperial system became more and more complete and thorough. Slow economic strangulation accompanied this relationship and the irony of former colonial power and ex-colonial territory in an economic alliance, joining hands to persecute the masses, is too sad to contemplate. The case of the Republic of Chad and France is instructive.

Imperialism depended and still depends on clear and unfettered channels of communication to further economic exploitation, just as colonialism formerly did. The wars between Spain, France, Holland and England in the seventeenth and eighteenth centuries were fought as much for the furtherance of trade, as for the domination of sea routes to pursue economic expansion.

25

Control of sea routes and therefore of channels of communication between metropolitan power and colonies was an integral part of the system. Without the certainty of the freedom to develop new markets and exploit new raw materials for the home industry, economic connection could not continue. In our own time, the monopoly of Agence Havas of the news agency business in Europe and the struggle of the Associated Press for entry into this lucrative market is an excellent example of the interaction of communication, economics and politics. More recently, the release of declassified documents enables us to understand the influence of economics, politics and communication in setting standards for television; more specifically, how France came to adopt its color television standards. 1/

The economic disequilibrium of the poor countries did not cease with the end of the colonial era, but accelerated. To the laisser faire theory of economic growth was added Ricardo's view of the division of labor: production should be encouraged in places where it was cheap to do so. This promoted agricultural and industrial development where the labor supply was cheap. Countries exported raw materials or goods in a semi-finished state to industrialized nations, which had the industrial capacity to convert them to finished products for exports. The consequence of international division of labor was not too difficult to see. Trade between the poor and the industrial countries increased, while trade between poor countries became less and less. Also, trade between industrialized countries was stimulated and continues to grow.

The volume of trade between the poor and developed countries is composed of primary products (most tend to have one major product, which can be exploited in commercial quantities; for example, bauxite in Jamaica, copper in Zambia). But goods sent to them, make up a comprehensive list of manufactures. Hence the dependency continued in a relationship which was more and more in favor of the developed countries, a relationship defined very much on their terms. The poor sell their products at market value and are subject to the fluctuations of the market. The cocoa industry provides copy: 2/

"[the industry]...saw the failure of a month-long United Nations-sponsored conference in

Geneva aimed at negotiating a new International Cocoa Agreement. The old agreement has never worked. The new meeting was inspired by consuming nations when supplies were down and prices were soaring, but even as the invitations were mailed a year ago, participants knew that conditions would be reversed by the time of the meeting--and that little would be accomplished."

A decline in price of primary products results in a weakening of economic strength and corresponding better terms of trade for rich countries. This economic domination is not a catch-as-catch can affair, but it is part of a deliberate policy designed to preserve the world dominion of capitalism. 3/

Economic domination falls into well-defined categories: control over money, including foreign exchange, public savings, when these are tied to loans from the imperialist powers; private savings and the control of mineral wealth by corporations which exploit them. Five main features of modern imperialism are identified: 4/ the setting up of structures to promote international capitalism; price regulation; union of state and private interests and multinational corporations and world banking agencies; sensitivity to the threat of socialism.

The total effect of this substantial economic imperialism was to convince the Third World that political independence is not to be confused with economic independence and political independence does not imply economic independence; indeed, the two are quite separate. Because of this Third World countries determined to initiate attempts to gain economic power as a means to enhance political independence.

The Third World came to realize that the so-called "free market" worked against their basic interests. They concluded that the market was not "free" at all and they could gain very little from it. They did not have the international leverage to bring about any conspicuous change. What they wanted was equality in terms of trade and not patronage and favors. Their collective viewpoint was echoed at Dakar in 1975, when they agreed to revise their approach to industrialized countries, stressing demands rather than entreaty and plea, which often amounted to indifference. 5/

This insensitivity has had a long history: mer-
cantilism, colonialism, imperialism, with each stage
having its own attendant economic frustration, brand of
servitude and nomenclature. The rich countries find it
difficult to describe the poor countries, either because of guilt, ignorance, or because the fluctuating
levels of poverty require a new vocabulary. Thus,
three different periods characterize their confusion,
each period with accompanying mythology: underdevelopment, development, Third World. Each period, locked in
its own embrace, as it were, contributes to the exclusion of creative possibilities for equal partnership,
thereby exacerbating frustrations.

Underdevelopment

This became a fashionable term to use in the postwar years, when the United States found itself the un-
disputed leader of the modern world, in terms of
wealth. The Marshall Plan, the North Atlantic Treaty
Organization (NATO), the South East Asia Treaty Organization (SEATO), attested to increasing influence and
the paranoia that resulted from it. Yet, there was an
interesting distinction between the description applied
to impoverished Europe, receiving the blessings of the
Marshall Plan and another country (say), India.

The most poverty-stricken European country,
Portugal, needed technical assistance and aid. India,
on the other hand, was underdeveloped. There is a
curious distinction. The former suggests transience
one in which misfortune played an overwhelming part
and in which somehow responsibility for the particular
situation (poverty) could not be taken. It implied
that forces outside that country were responsible for
the state in which it found itself. It was very easy
in the European case to blame Germany, which was for
the most part easily identifiable. Europe, the victim
of Nazi aggression, had to be helped to her feet again.
It was easier for the United States to identify with
Europe than with Asia. But the same sympathy did not
occur with countries, which were also victims of aggression in a no less destructive form: economic aggression. It little mattered that in economic terms
Europe at that time shared with much of the rest of
the world a poverty of resource. Europe qualified
therefore for an aid program, a connotation that became
synonymous with relief, a temporary inconvenience
rather than a permanent state.

28

That permanent state was reserved for non-European countries, two-thirds of the rest of the world, whom Michael Harrington calls, the "vast majority." They became associated in the American mind as a permanent condition: the underdeveloped condition. Underdevelopment suggests resistance to change, an inherent backwardness; and as most of these countries are non-European, it is conceivable that racial stereotyping became a correlative of the development process. These countries became therefore objects of patronage at best, and creatures of exploitation at worse.

Characteristic of this period are high interest rates, development plans that had little bearing on what these countries could afford, costly impractical schemes, hosts of resident experts and oppressive bureaucratic machinery, irrelevant to the tasks of real development. The guru of the time, Walt Rostow, whose Stages of Economic Development, categorized development according to fixed economic stages, provided justification for the Establishment.

Underdevelopment signified paralysis of the human condition that could not be motivated even in its own self-interest, and hence a worthy object of contempt. This attitude was not actually stated, but it was all the more prevalent because it was not. And for those who would deny this, it is well to remember that psychological attitudes are as much a part of development as economic policies and very often the former influence the latter. 6/

But the "underdeveloped" countries began to understand the international ramifications of development, and reacted to increased possibilities for influence and competition on the international market. In many respects, the very denial of aid and the unfavorable terms on which it was obtained, when it was obtained, stimulated a competitive and nationalist spirit. For example, Nyerere of Tanzania, refused to be blackmailed by the government of West Germany into accepting the Hallstein doctrine, which forbade recognition of communist East Germany, on pain of cutting off all development aid programs.

Aid programs have suffered from an embarrassment of tribulations. Mistakes, poor administration, and chaos have sometimes accompanied them. In some instances, aid was used to prop up unpopular regimes, as in Santo Domingo, and also regimes which had lost

29

the support of the country, or had no support at all
to begin with. Also, many of the built-in structural
weaknesses of institutions in donor countries were
transferred to "underdeveloping" countries, with the
result that the institutions of the latter became car-
bon copies of shaky originals.

Many of these countries could not sustain such
assaults on their institutions and they opposed what
they considered as exploitation by other means. Unfortunately, however, to change one source of exploitation was no guarantee against similar treatment elsewhere. They realized that though industrially and technologically advanced countries might differ politically,
they did not differ substantially, when it came to their
own national interests. Political ideology was therefore no guide to conduct.

For example, aid programs might be tied to specific requests (demands?) for changes in the host countries; and if these requests were based on inadequate
information, or scanty, or superficial knowledge of
local conditions, they further compounded an unfortunate circumstance. Furthermore, increasing quantities of aid added to the national debt (since very
little aid is given in grants) and depleted already
limited foreign exchange. What the rich gave with one
hand, they took with the other.

One of the areas not often touched on in analyses
of foreign aid is the 'gift' of institutional structures. A convincing case can be and often is presented
for administrative machinery to direct and supervise
aid programs; and certainly, there is evidence that administration of complex and expensive programs might
best be conducted through specific offices set up for
this purpose. Too often procedures presided over by
a dispirited, complicated bureaucracy composed of
poorly paid, disgruntled civil servants, could not
function either at maximum efficiency or speed. Then,
too extensive aid programs demanded varying degrees of
responses, which understaffed and not always competent
government departments, were not in a position to administer. But streamlining began when it was found
that the host country had to pay the costly expenses
of maintenance out of the funds loaned.

Examples of this kind abound. Host countries set
their expectations too high, only to be disillusioned;
and donor countries, with much vaunted optimism have

had their hopes dashed.

"Underdevelopment" was as much an attitude of mind
that obsessed both donor and host. Each became locked
in and imprisoned within the psychological limits.
Neither could immediately break from the shackles in
which it found itself. The donor could not resist feeling that he was aiding the unfortunate and the host
could not also help support the misery that obligation
and patronage entailed, as well as the financial
squeeze which this sometimes represented. The German
word "entwicklungshelfer" (development aid) comes
closest to bringing out the psychological attributes
of the process. Indeed, the German Ministry of Economic Development ran a campaign (1965-68) to try to rid
the pejorative associations behind the term development aid, which, of course, implied underdevelopment
and insufficiency.

This period coincided with moves internationally
for a new approach to development aid, or at least a
redefinition of the old ideas. It was not only to ful-
fill their own still narrowly defined ends, but also
because it was simply a more efficient tactic for aid,
exploitation and mutual self-interest. Much more could
be exacted from a relationship on both counts, if the
operation ran smoothly and efficiently. There was
every apparent reason for this.

A plethora of studies confirmed that the wealth
of many developing countries was as yet untapped and a
whole mine of resources was there waiting for exploitation. These countries suffered from lack of capital,
manpower and general industrial know-how essential for
development. They desired and looked for new markets;
and as they were suspicious in some cases of traditional markets (some former colonial territories tended
this way, while others re-embraced their former colonial masters with renewed energies--the Ivory Coast and
France, for example), they eagerly sought out new opportunities in Japan and West Germany. Both sides
agreed that much could be gained from a new relationship, or at least a rethinking of the old. Aid, despite the unfortunate associations, and exploitative
nature, had in some cases done much good work.

What was needed then was a new philosophy to enhance exploitation, development, and altruism, dis-
guising each in proportion to commitment and specific
undertaking, and achieving some measure of success,

31

individual or collective. Idealism was found to be the ingredient, measured doses of which could both conceal intentions, hide motives as well as perform capable tasks. The several bands of young people, the various Peace Corps' of different and differing varieties in diverse lands, contributed enormously to the renewed images of donor countries, revitalizing tired and worn impressions of earlier time.

Extensive briefings, including language learning for new trainees to administer aid programs, the involvement of universities on the planning level, helped the new image, which became one of liberalism in deed if not in thought. Increased participation of the young and the skilled attracted and encouraged many more to take part in numerous projects spanning the globe. In keeping with the new philosophical approach, a new image was devised, promoted and popularized through the mass media of communication.

Relationships between donor and host countries therefore came easier with a redefinition of status. A practiced sensitivity by donor countries ensured, partly at any rate, that development would progress smoothly. Responsible for this change was the psychological attitude to the process of development. Underdevelopment became development. "Underdeveloping" countries became developing countries.

Development

Development was seen as a process that incorporated both donor and host in surprising ways. Donor countries realized that they had as much to gain out of their investment as the host countries. Systems theory encouraged widespread use of a spectra of variables to amplify the developing process. Developing operations became part of the concerns, if not the trappings, of any country that could afford to be in the business. What formerly used to be the occupation of a senior civil servant, operating out of a cubbyhole, became a vast operation within the portfolio of a tried government minister and armies of bureaucratic paraphernalia in close attendance.

Development became a study in and for itself. Graduate schools at the time, anxious to expand, quickly picked up the general direction of government interest (most received some form of federal allocations for research in the life and behavioral sciences,

32

which made it easier to ascertain the direction of government interests). As a result organizations like the Agency for International Development, could draw on many young and eager graduates to swell the ranks of its expert staff. The same was true in France, England and Germany.

Universities interfaced with governments and training of one kind or another accompanied gentle government prodding. This had two results. First, it provided an expert coterie of intelligent and in some cases learned, though untried, opinion on which governments and foundations could draw. Second, governments could be assured of alternative blueprints for some projects, of a more than adequate testing ground for theories, and also random eclecticism from whatever quarter it came. And not least of the results of the emphasis on development was the increased cooperation between governments, private foundations and corporations, each with its own hierarchy of excellence, which was at times interchangeable, and interchanged. The case of Robert S. McNamara is instructive. An executive at the Ford Foundation, he moved to Defence Secretary and finally to the presidency of the International Bank for Reconstruction and Development (the World Bank).

In the U.S., three distinct phases of development might be traced in the national psyche: the 1940s, when aid was wrapped up in the Mutual Security Act, the 1950s, when a policy of economic development began to be fashioned more in keeping with the world realities and 1960s, when this policy was executed through the Foreign Assistance Act. The Marshall Plan by which European reconstruction was supported, represented the apex of development planning, which has not been since equalled; and the objective conditions which existed for the success of any aid program were ideally matched with regard to Europe. 7/

Economic development was increasingly seen during the middle fifties and the early sixties less as a moral imperative, than as a security consideration. In fact, the current direction of all aid is progressively towards security considerations. The literature of our times has tended to overstress moral considerations, perhaps out of a desire to conceal the real motives to action, or else to placate guilt, and while it is true that a spirit of solidarity among nations and peoples has developed over the postwar years, it is unnecessary to overemphasize it where it does exist, or to assume it, where it does not. In any case national interests take precedence when they have to, and the spirit of solidarity vanishes as though it never existed.

Apart from security, political factors have also conspicuously influenced development. Aid has been given to a friendly government to stem a crisis, e.g., Brazil, 1964, to help a government win elections, e.g., Chile, 1964 and 1971, and El Salvador, 1983. On the other hand, aid has been cut off from those governments which perpetrated acts against established policy.

Development is based on assessed needs, real or imagined. Poor countries lack and therefore need hard currency to conduct international trade, to purchase equipment and supplies to carry out modest, and sometimes not so modest, national goals. Rich countries have exchanged this for political as well as economic benefits. The U.S., for example, has sought to extend its influence over the South American hemisphere. France has successfully managed to preserve its influence among the former West African colonies by a series of international agreements, including the European Common Market, and the Lome Convention.

Development assistance has not therefore been unambiguous. It has been mixed with very pointed and concerned national interests, security considerations and political involvements.

Development aid benefits both donor and recipient, if not in the short-run, then eventually, but at a price. Security considerations are of uncertain value and tend to fluctuate as national policies change, and factors which influence national policy are many. Political factors are of increasing concern and tend to be as variable as questions of security, for it is often the case that a new government administration redefines its priorities. 8/ Also, policies of the host countries sometimes affect the donor countries. For example, when the Republic of Guinea chose independence in 1958, it affected the quality and amount of French aid; likewise, the nationalization of bauxite by the Republic of Guyana brought a change in its relations with the United States and Canada.

Other problems too frustrate the aid process. The distribution of aid in particular is a field requiring much experience and expertise. Also, within host countries administrators often discriminate between various aid projects, singling out those for attention which more directly support their own interests, at the expense of others, which might be more advantageous for the country.

Development aid is not altruistic. And national interests and paternalism define relations between donor and host countries. The former is right in calling for stability as a condition for development aid, but the latter is also right in contending that aid can be vital in creating the conditions for stability.

The complaint usually heard in the Third World is that donor countries not only want to be the piper, but they also want to call the tune. These considerations cannot be divorced from those of costs and the financial involvement in aid programs. For instance, technical assistance not only includes equipment but also expertise, human resources, considerable bureaucracy and high administrative overhead, which poor countries are expected to bear, as well as high salaries and other fringe benefits. These are part of the agenda of development aid for institution building, which can cause estrangement between donor and host and frustrate the very aims that are to be accomplished.

Development also touches equally sensitive areas. Donor countries have increasingly sought to tie aid programs to specific orders or commitments viz the purchase of materials and equipment from certain firms within their countries. These commitments have imposed a severe limitation on the financial flexibility of poor countries, which must forego other competitive markets because of these agreements. The result is that the poor countries become involved in an ever deepening morass of debts and balance of payments difficulties.

The demands of national development entailed a willingness to explore all avenues for aid and assistance and at the most favorable conditions possible. But no such clarity enveloped the psyche of the donor countries, which viewed the entire development aid situation with a mixture of motives. "We help you but we also help ourselves, or at least not hinder ourselves," may be a good way of putting it. And if, as sometimes inevitably happens, trading arrangements threaten, or appear to threaten, traditional economic hegemony, then governments overreact and threaten reprisals. For example, the Nixon administration made clear...to developing countries that they can expect no general trade preferences if their trading pacts with the European Economic Community discriminate against American goods." 9/

Development aid to poor countries is based not only on economic interests but also on moral, security and political considerations. The moral argument rested rather heavily, but temporarily, on the shoulders of the Kennedy Frontiersmen, who clearly derived much comfort from the belief that "those who have should share with those who have not." This reasoning as a working program for development aid did not lend itself so easily to foreign policy objectives and could not endure the rigors of national self-interest.

A wide and sometimes increasing disparity of development priorities confused both donor and host countries. Levels of expectation sometimes were too high for the immediate objectives of the programs. Because of the newness of development aid, the countries involved had no backlog of experience on which to draw, causing unpredictable results at best and confusion at worst. Rich countries often expected the poor countries to be grateful for their attention and often noticeably cooled if this was not the case.

The result was that there was a marked lessening of development aid for this and other reasons. The humanitarian psyche, which had clothed the earlier efforts, was replaced by a more pragmatic, and some would argue, a more exploitative policy. Development aid came to be defined more strictly in concert with the interests of the State; and poor countries, which were not of obvious interest, either from strategic or economic considerations, could claim no high priority. For example, France's aid to her former possessions in West Africa assumed a commitment, which was in keeping with its political ambitions. The moral argument for aid became weakened because of the seeming difficulty of spreading the cake all round and giving each his share of the pie--some were apt to want more than their fair share--and donor countries were themselves unable to effectively control the distribution; the apparatus set up for this purpose, was not up to its demands.

Other reasons too, brought about a change. Development aid was associated with the aftermath of the Cold War and the climate of suspicion that prevailed between Western and Eastern powers. They began to compete for the rights to divide the spoils. The battle for black Africa was enjoined. This was also to have an effect on the host countries, which not slow to capitalize on this increased attention, flirted now with one side and then the other, and occasionally, like Sri Lanka, with both sides. Also, these poor countries began to flex their muscles.

There was the first Bandung conference in April 1955, when the first tentative steps towards coordination of policies were taken. The word "non-aligned" was coined, symbolizing more what they did not want than what they wanted. A kind of precarious unity began to develop and the United Nations was the forum for it. Gradually, a pattern developed and countries, united more by what they did not have, than what they did have, appeared on the world stage. To a greater extent, a precarious harmony crystallized around Vietnam, and they identified with what was generally considered to be the victim of capitalist aggression, in much the same way that earlier they had identified and still do with Cuba. The economic realities of their condition seemed to improve them, or at least, to universalize the knowledge of their plight. This assorted array of countries saw itself as sharing a very special kind of experience: deprivation and poverty.

The halo surrounding the word development underwent change, even though the word persisted to haunt those who had not translated it into definite policy. Likewise also, the poor countries, which had been the recipients of economic attention for two decades, redefined their strategies for dealing with new factors, and changing world realities. They became the concern of the Third World.

The Third World

Imprecise in terminology and inadequately defined, the Third World has come to generally symbolize all the have-not countries. Conceived as a reproach to the rich countries, it demonstrates an awakening, a new consciousness among the exploited, united by similar historical circumstance.

Within this group there are contradictions. They
do not all have the same political philosophy. Their
attitudes to the rich countries are not all the same.
There is no firm agreement which binds them to matters
affecting them. They might more easily be defined in
terms of their economy and economic relations with rich
countries. Their energy and fuel consumption is low:
their trade is mainly directed towards rich countries.
Conditions of life are far below even the minimum
standards established by organizations such as UNESCO;
life expectancy is low, diet is inadequate and so is
medical care. Yet these same countries occupy half the
earth's surface and approximately two-thirds its population.

This pitiable and unenviable condition of the
Third World is not without a certain virtue. The realization that one is poor is perhaps the first necessary
step for the elimination of poverty. The United Nations
Development Fund, the popularization of conditions in
the Third World by the mass media of communication,
stimulated interest in a world made closer by rapid
communication. Above all, many realized that no country could remain isolated from world problems for long
if it valued its own security. The price of survival
was dependency to some degree.

Among the rich countries, strategy for dealing
with this new challenge began to be mapped. But it became clear that the interrelation of many was not to
be at the expense of the few, or to put it bluntly,
relations between the Third World was not to interfere
with continued exploitation. Among Third World countries, some strength was derived from the knowledge that
they were not alone in their plight. This conscious
awareness of exploitation was responsible for a profound change in their disposition.

The Third World saw the awesome connection between
national power, the multinational corporation and international political manipulation. Recent history
abounds with the philandering of the tripartite phalanx, operating in the defense of their own interests.
A significant consequence of this was an examination
of the structure, functions and performance of the mass
media of communication. More specifically, the question asked was: are the mass media agents of the system which continues to exploit? Assaults on the Western press must be seen as part of the overall concerns

that its role, however carefully defined in philosophical niceties, is ambiguous and replete with contradiction.

Increasingly, therefore, the Third World began to see themselves as victims and the rich countries as aggressors. One of the features of the aggressor is that its expansionist aims puts it in an aggressive and defensive role at one and the same time. That is to say, it must create new markets and these markets once obtained, must be defended at whatever the cost. This duality, while it creates the climate for aggression on an increasing scale, also supports a schizophrenia that believes it is under attack when it is not, threatened when it is not--presumably, because aggression must be prepared for the eventuality of aggression.

Primarily, it is because the Third World hovers on the verge of revolutionary ambitions, which can only be at the expense of the rich, or so it seems to them. It is therefore a threat to the status quo, and therefore to be rooted out, where such designs raise their ugly head and restrained before they infect the world body politic. To wit, the Pentagon spends a billion dollars annually on a communications system to warn against "trouble" in the Third World. 10/ The U.S. invasion of Grenada is an illuminating example of reaction to a perceived hemispheric threat.

If there is a suggestion that rich countries have become disenchanted with the affairs of the Third World in general, then that suggestion is true. In fact, it might lie in one area of agreement shared by the Right and the Left; that Third World countries should fend for themselves and that development aid should be channelled through international organizations as a safety valve against obvious risks such as revolution, nationalization, seizure and other uncomfortable expectations.

The roots of this disenchantment with the Third World are many and no one particular factor is responsible. To begin with, the Third World has become increasingly militant and aggressive and a Congressman or a British Member of Parliament would find himself embarrassed to explain or to defend the need for development aid to a local constituency, aware only of the latest affront of (say) Ecuador to his country. Second, economic development has seemed not to keep pace with population growth and planners and experts have become pessimistic. Third, expectations were particularly high that aid would accomplish more than it did in fact. Finally, the Third World itself began to experience a measure of disenchantment, when it discovered that development aid was not really aid, but a business investment camouflaged to look like development aid.

Still, however, development aid persists because the reasons for it to persist are greater than the reasons for it not to. Put another way, as long as development aid benefits, there is every reason why it will continue, even though the rewards might not be as great as anticipated. In any case, it is difficult to measure or to calculate the exact amount of benefits, especially when some of these are hidden. And in order to ensure that their influence does persist in the Third World, the rich countries have devised a number of clever strategies which deserve some attention.

Strategies for continued influence

First, the institutionalizing of aid programs through international bodies set up as a buffer between them and the Third World. These cushion the blow if it falls too hard and also allow the rich to involve themselves in a less direct way in the affairs of other states. International coverage facilitates their intervention at all levels in affairs, without prejudice to their position or without jeopardizing national prestige. It also allows them to influence, if not direct the future course of events inside the Third World, using the institution as a convenient camouflage. The recommendation of the Jackson Report, advocating increased centralization of the United Nations Development Programme (UNDP), must be seen as a means by which control of that Programme can be achieved by a country sufficiently wealthy to be able to. 11/

Second, closely allied to this, is the attitude of mind which partnership suggests. Unwilling to admit that wealth defines status in the world, rich countries have allowed themselves the luxury of believing that they can work in partnership with the Third World, thus seeking to create the illusion of equality. Only equals can be partners. There is little that an Indian peasant in the altiplano of Bolivia can have in common with an expert who advises him on nutrition. The notion that unequals can be partners is presumptious and paternalistic. Indeed, paternalism on the one hand and exploitation on the other, might be said to be the chief characteristics of most aid programs, though it would be idle to deny that despite this, they do bring some benefit when properly administered.

Partnership is also extended relationship, as governments work in concert with private agencies, each supporting the other. The Overseas Private Investment Corporation set up in 1970 during the Nixon administration, managed to combine both public and private officials. The ITT scandal in Chile is an example of how government can support a multinational corporation and how close the potentiality there is for danger because of it. 12/

Increased development opportunities, greater participation in international affairs, increased aid programs, profusion of reports and studies, reveal a new concern with Third World countries. But they also display a new fear; that somehow if the rich do not take part (intervene?) then they do so at their own peril. They need to keep a watchful eye to see that they do not in anyway imperil their standards of living; and primary products like oil can affect and paralyze any economy. Rich countries are also well aware of the potentiality of future markets of Third World countries. They realize, too, that in a shrinking world, they cannot insulate themselves from currents that might blow from that direction. This is so for three reasons.

First, the speed at which modern communications promote social interaction, irrespective of the ideology, has forced some governments to keep in step with the concerns of their citizens. For example, the pressure exerted internationally by those governments whose citizens had become targets for hijackers. Second, the likelihood of military conflicts breaking out in Third World countries and causing wider involvement. Finally, because international relations have become both interwoven and complex; dependence and interdependence are part of the same matrix of responsibility, obligation and cooperation: nuclear disarmament, the law of the sea and satellite and outer space relations affect all countries.

41

But the concern is that this renewed interest, based on assorted data, do not conceal the main thesis; that is, that the rich have at hand a hegemony, notwithstanding noble intentions, which is used to dominate, particularly in the economic and cultural fields, and further their interests.

Underdevelopment, development and the Third World roughly correspond to various strategies of communication and development. Much of the research, particularly in academia, which is always a useful barometer for national attitudes, shows this. These three "psyches" are essentially stages in the mythology of development and modernization. To become modern is to reflect the institutions of technologically advanced countries, without the safeguards from exploitation, which attends the modernization process. 13/ Modernization is really an amalgam of three basic conditions: economic growth; institutional development; and technical and managerial sophistication. Information and communication strategies are components for efficiency in modernization.

Communication and development

Economic development is crucial to this transformation and also the role of the mass media in national development, which is "really a broad transformation of society." 14/ As part of this general movement, national consciousness must be aroused. With a concerted national consciousness, the problems of development can be spiritedly attacked. Productivity is essential and increased productivity means money for investment--money which can be obtained from savings or borrowing. The former clearly is to be preferred to the latter. Productivity is to be achieved in the industrial sector, but not at the expense of agriculture; and one of the characteristics of underdevelopment is the low profitability of agriculture.

Both agriculture and industry need the support of infrastructure, communications, power, transport. Also, without the mobilization of human resources through education, skills, health, and housing, national development is not likely to be comprehensive. Development plans have carefully reflected this trend, supporting a broad strategy of mobilization. Productivity must be ahead of population growth in order for economic growth to take place and population gains can frustrate what the country gains from investment.

42

Productivity from investment is central to the economist's position.

But in order to invest in industry, agriculture and social overhead must be considered as top priorities. Agriculture influences industrial development and the latter supports agricultural development. But here is the rub. Agricultural development in traditional societies is a difficult process, requiring money, education and the teaching of skills. Above all, it requires an attitude of mind which would rid itself from the shackles of an unproductive mode of existence and be ready to try new technology. This is where the mass media of communication becomes involved. Information which is necessary for this transformation, can be disseminated by the mass media as they mobilize human resources.

As part of mobilization of human resources, people must be exposed to new ways of doing things, and they must be presented with information and learn from the attainments of societies outside of their own. Information and its flow inevitably raise questions about rights and responsibilities. Information is never value-free and mirrors the political philosophy of the administration in power, or the country from which it comes.

Granted a country decides to modernize and is seriously prepared to undergo this transformation process, the ethics of the process of modernization becomes one for that country to decide. It is quite evident that national development involves a restructuring of society and inevitably the whole society becomes involved in this, whether it wants to or not. In order for development to be comprehensive, certain choices must be made, depending on the amount of information available.

The Western position is that the free flow of information is a desirable feature in and for itself, and one which enhances choice. Lack of free flow of information is held to restrict choice. It is for this reason that a free press is desirable for itself but even more so as an instrument of the development process. The free flow of information enables people to participate in the decision-making process. It also permits information to circulate so that cities and rural areas keep in touch and know what the other is doing. Also, of equal importance is the adequacy of channels for communication. Ideally, societies should ensure that there are sufficient channels for communication to convey messages essential for economic and social development, for in this way, leaders and communities can learn more about one another. The former understands the needs of the latter who are informed about the policies of the administration and what they are expected to do.

Because development depends for its effectiveness on a planned working relationship between experts, people and administration, theories were advanced, advocating specific uses for the mass media. All had one characteristic in common: an overrated belief in the infallibility of the mass media as agents of change. Many there were who preached the glories of television in the cause of education, health, information etc., and went along sublimely advising governments of their certainty. Few caveats were adhered to and the boundless enthusiasm marched strongly into the seventies with hardly a false step. 15/

Emphasis was placed squarely on hardware, and other components of the system viz persons and environment were blissfully ignored. And certainly there were areas where the mass media (despite the bias towards hardware) did contribute. For example, the mass media did stimulate awareness in societies; they did contribute towards national consciousness; they did provide more information about many aspects of life beyond the experiences of many societies. But the mass media also contributed to a misguided certainty that developmental problems would vanish overnight and the consequent euphoria, which facts did not sustain.

The mass media do help, do contribute to national development, but their assistance in this regard must be tempered by the reality and acknowledgement that they help in company with, or together with, other elements, which comprise interpersonal communications. There is very little justification for a cause-effect relationship in the social sciences.

The net result of this apparent failure of the mass media to satisfy the ambitions of the Third World was to further alienate them from the source of a technology, which promised more than it delivered.

The alienation resulted in policy considerations being taken more seriously. The "overnight" expert made way for the comprehensive plan in which international cooperation became more visible in the fields of information and development: The Agency for International Development (AID), and the Canadian Agency for International Development (CIDA), among others, expanded their development efforts in many countries and the United Nations Development Programme (UNDP) developed policies for information and development.

UNDP outlined two components for the role of information and development: program support information and development information. Both of these components were endorsed by UNESCO in 1971 as part of its operational program and its department of mass communications stressed the need for both components to be developed within the country itself and with external aid.

The establishment of a communications infrastructure which had been considered a vital part of UNESCO's First Development Decade had shown that there was a greater need for a more comprehensive policy to bridge the gap between urban and rural areas. But the results of the First Development Decade had shown the need for a comprehensive communications policy. 16/

National communications policy

In the guarded language that punctuates official documents from that world organization, there is more than a hint of dissatisfaction with results of the communication policies. It became clear during the Second Development Decade that the role of the mass media did not live up to expectations. 17/ National communication policies were the inevitable result of the failure of a system of free choice and became an alternative to a limited and inadequate view of communication.

The trend towards national communications policies is neither hasty nor casual. Rather, it is a recognition that the earlier enthusiasm for the sanctity of communications in the development process was misplaced, and the modest results required drastic revision in strategy. More to the point, national communications policies represent a rejection of certain persistent ideas of the role of the mass media in the development process. These ideas are not

45

divorced from the mainstream of thought about the Third World by industrialized countries. Three media perspectives are identified: colonial, technocratic and hegemonic. 18/

The colonial view is all too familiar and needs no embellishment or critical study: that it still persists is as much an indictment against both colonial power and colonized.

The technocratic view seeks to understand the Third World by reference to its approximation to Western technology. (The closer you are the better.) Accordingly, the emphasis here is on strict materialism, with quantitative indices within the GNP, budgetary considerations, communications portfolio, including number of radio and television sets and cinema seats per thousand and what these indicate for the development process. International agencies were quick to see the correlation between modernization, the desirability for materialism and the equation between quantity and development. The view still is current, although in some restricted form, and with it the notion that economic development is the sole area for mass media application.

The above supposition is that modernization equals material and technical resources; and as this equation generally is true for industrialized countries, it is believed to hold for the Third World. This emphasis on materialism can be seen in an attendant field such as educational technology, where an early focus on the technical apparatus has given way (blessedly) to the systems approach for viewing the learning process.

The final perspective, the hegemonic, considers any substantive change as threatening to the status quo and therefore dangerous. The U.S. press war against Allende's government in Chile derives from this view; 19/ also, the attitudes of the U.S. press and the cold war are of similar currency. 20/

Third World Anguish

Thus, the roots of Third World distress rest not only in the misery of economic inadequacy, the perpetuation of stereotypic models, which conform to ethnocentric ideas, but also in the frustrations inherent in the modernization process itself. Western attitudes are important, for collectively, the Western

46

industrialized countries are large investors in the
modernizing process in the Third World.

But the issue of survival in the Third World is
related to, though it does not entail, modernization.
For example, a society where traditional authority is
sacred may find itself unable to completely accept the
idea of free speech and individual freedom of action.
Culture, rooted in tradition, acts as a restraining
influence on personal initiative, a feature of modernization. The individual hovers between adherence to
a world of his upbringing and that to which he must
adapt, in the interests of progress and survival.

It is the need to survive, in what is increasingly looked upon as a hostile environment, in which economic impotence is fast becoming bitterness, that
militates Third World countries, by no means united
ideologically, economically, politically, causing them
to consider common strategy.

One of the earliest conferences to identify the
roots of the problem and how it manifested itself, at
least in Africa, was the All-African People's Conference in Cairo in 1961. But sensitivity, allied to such
action which at the time they could take, did not succeed in obtaining any substantial economic gains. In
the interim such palliatives as GATT, UNCTAD could
devise, and development aid of one sort or another
from many countries served but to strengthen inequality. But it was the failure of the two Development
Decades, which were grandiose attempts to focus resources and attention on Third World development, that
resulted in much unease and loss of confidence.

The New International Economic Order was born out
of Third World bitterness at the inability of the institutions which regulate international trade and com-
merce to share their bounty and the failure also of
attempts to improve living conditions. At the root of
the problem are the institutions of the market system
which control terms of trade, making it impossible
for poor countries to participate fully in the economic
system. Institutions create and promote dependency.

Thus, the view gained credence that the free market is not free at all and works for and in the interests of the rich. This imbalance systematically
discriminates against the poor, denying them equality
of opportunity in world markets.

47

The ideas behind the New International Economic Order are noble and must be seen in terms of economic survival of the Third World, in much the same way that the non-aligned movement must be seen as a movement towards political independence and an alternative to power blocs. That both rest on fragile foundations, does not in any detract from the justice of their cause. The reality of "two-thirds of mankind living on less than thirty cents a day...70 per cent of the children in the Third World suffering from malnutrition...millions of people toiling under a broiling sun from morning till dusk for miserable rewards and premature death without ever discovering the reasons why...," 21/ must give pause to the world's major statesmen.

That the NIEO is not seen with burning passion by rich countries as a way of sharing is due partly to how the concept is sold. The mass media, which essentially defend the very interests that would have to make the "sacrifices," do not treat the matter sufficiently seriously in the view of the Third World. When they do, it is to point out the difficulties, or in some cases to ridicule the idea altogether. Debate and discussion is altogether limited and the seriousness of the question is confined to the halls of academia, which have always been the place where impractical ideas of this sort are hatched.

The NIEO is a victim of its sweeping recommendations, which appear to disturb the economic balance now weighed heavily against the poor. Change always upsets societies and the comprehensive change envisaged by the NIEO deeply disturbs the rich. They feel threatened by it. They believe that to share their goods would bring about a decline in their standard of living, causing them to be less than prosperous. Accustomed to pursuing selfish national interests, they are reluctant to redress "global inequities" through international action. Moreover, they are unwilling to admit that the NIEO is the minimum requirement for a stable and just international world.

But these recommendations are not radical at all. The distinguished Dutch economist, Jan Tinbergen, coordinated a group of specialists to consider the worldwide implications of the world's present and future needs. The simplicity of the statement conceals an avalance of very deep and abiding concerns, which divide the world and about which it is most preoccupied: the armaments race, population, food, human

48

settlements, environment, international monetary and trading systems; natural resources and energy; science and technology; transnational enterprises; the ocean; outerspace; international institutions; and planetary interdependencies.

Tinbergen's Report establishes a need for a new international order and justifies its findings, ranging over wide areas and including a succinct treatment of how the various economies deal with national problems. That which appears to be a modest prescription for reform, has not met with universal acclaim, and many who pay lip-service in public are not prepared to go further. A plan which calls for a capitalist solution to world problems remains unsupported by capitalists.

Many in the Third World interpret this as an unwillingness to participate fully in the development process and also as a deliberate effort on the part of the rich to maintain technical and scientific superiority. The more plain spoken call attention to the vista of forces against which they must contend in order to achieve some limited prosperity for their people. Arraigned against them are the national and international banks, the transnational corporations spawning a multitude of enterprises, including international bodies and a world system, which like a hydra-headed monster envelopes them.

The world system is revealed not only in monopoly capitalism, which they always knew about, but in other areas as well (which they suspected but had little evidence to support their suspicions). One consequence of this world system is the identification of various sectors of the planning stage with one another and the interrelation of parts. Thus, economic development and information is the prop which supports and drives the mechanism of science and technology. The relation of economics to information strategy is a dynamic one.

The Third World sees that a broad attack must be made against the supports of the world system: Information and the channels through which it passes, is a target for assault: radio, television and film, the channels of communication, which daily attack their living space; the news agencies, which they hold accountable for interpreting news about them with little sympathy or understanding; the advertising

49

agencies, whose messages leave them vulnerable to foreign influences and distort reality; cheap books and
magazines, which occasionally expose them to ridicule;
above all, the transnational corporations with their
infinite resources of sophisticated communication systems from data banks, computers to satellites supported
by governments. How can a market system which is not
free purport to have free media institutions. To phrase
the question differently: can a free press exist in an
economic system that is not free.

The catalogue of complaints is interminable, sometimes approaching paranoia. But it does represent the
extent of the bitterness and distress that the Third
World suffers as a result of the endless cycle of
poverty and despair. It is to some of these specific
charges that we now turn.

Notes

1/ Crane, R.J. The Problems of International Standards. Norwood, N.J.: Ablex Publishing Corporation, 1979.

2/ The New York Times, February 26, 1979.

3/ Fann, K.T. and D.C. Hodges. Readings in U.S. Imperialism. Boston: Porter Sargent Publishers, 1971.

4/ O'Connor, J. "The meaning of economic imperialism." In Fann & Hodges (eds.), Readings in U.S. Imperialism, op. cit., 1971.

5/ Reshaping the International Order. A Report to the Club of Rome. New York: E.P. Dutton, 1976.

6/ McLelland, D. The Achieving Society. Cambridge: Harvard University Press, 1962.

7/ Hunter, R.E. & Rielly, J.E. Development Today. New York: Praeger Publishers, 1972.

8/ The Alliance that lost its way. A critical report of the Alliance for Progress. Washington, D.C., 1970.

9/ The New York Times, April 6, 1973.

10/ Schiller, H. Op. cit., 1969.

11/ Hazzard, S. Defeat of an Ideal. Boston: Little Brown, 1973.

12/ Onimode, B. "Imperialism and Multinational Corporations." Journal of Black Studies. Vol. 9, No. 2, Dec. 1978.

13/ Moore, W. E. Social Change. Englewood Cliffs: Prentice Hall, N.J., 1965.

14/ Schramm, W. Mass Media and National Development. Stanford: Stanford University Press, 1964.

15/ Oettinger, A. Run, computer, run. New York: Collier Books, 1969.

16/   Naesselund, G.   Op. cit., 1977.

17/   Evaluation by the Director-General of the Results of the First Development Decade, UNESCO, Paris, 1970.

18/   Pollock, J. C.   An Anthropological Approach to Mass Communications Research.   Latin American Research Review.   Vol. 13, No. 1, 1978.

19/   Aronson, J.   The Press and the Cold War.   New York: Bobbs-Merrill, 1970.

20/   Reshaping the International Order.   Report to the Club of Rome.   New York: E.P. Dutton, Publishers, 1976.

21/   Gans, H.   Deciding What's News.   New York: Pantheon, 1979.

Chapter 3

LITANY OF THIRD WORLD COMPLAINTS

These are varied, substantial, basically psychological and reflect powerlessness. The litany of
complaints is all the more real, even if it may be
senseless to Western ears.

There are undeniable virtues in the practice and
performance of Western media. The pursuit of objectivity, which is not to be confused with its practice,
the striving for accuracy, the search for a modus
vivendi beyond reach of government and governing administrations, are proclaimed purposes, with which few
would cavil. But these are noble intentions, which
must be seen as an on-going process rather than an at-
tainable end, which, in a philosophical sense, makes
of the journalist a skeptic, sharing with the philo-
sopher, the search for meaning and definition.

For much of the time, therefore, the journalist
is a seeker after truth, groping in the darkness,
piecing together the torn fragments of reality, re-
constituting the canvas so that it bears some resem-
blance to the original. In the process he uses training skills, an analytical frame of mind, a psychological and cultural background and the ready perceptions
which accompany his work. The written story, the edi-
ted television report, the recorded interview then becomes his version of an event in the newspaper, the
wire services, the radio and television broadcast. But
it is not a facsimile of the event, for there can be
none such. Every attempt at facsimile is doomed and
what emerges is the reporter's reconstruction of the
event. Objectivity is therefore impossible, but the
pursuit of it is. In fact, it is highly dangerous
and misleading to speak of objectivity in absolute
terms. To do so is to deceive the reporter (assuming
he has not already deceived himself about what he is
doing), and dupe the public about what it is reading
or viewing.

Yet this deception of the public is administered
with a great deal of thoroughness and care by those
who wish to perpetuate the myth of objectivity. This
peculiar myth dies hard in Western societies, which
continue to hold fast to it. The assorted news establishments, including the wire services, broadcast

networks, national as well as regional and local newspapers help perpetuate it; schools of journalism which
feed students the belief to assure its continuity;
communication departments of major universities, which
pay scrupulous attention to the textbook empire; and
worn out academics, who have long lost the habit of
thinking creatively. The adherents of the myth of
objectivity ensure that its righteousness persists and
that it stands as the benchmark of journalism. The
reasons for this are curious and bear some examination.

First, objectivity is bound up with a society's
progress towards collective virtue. In a changing age
to be objective is to safeguard truth, the one reality
that changes not, is immutable and undestructive. It
is a logical hangover from Greek philosophy, which considered objectivity as the guardian of truth and the
cornerstone of civic rectitude; and the virtue which
withstood barbarism was held to be its own just reward.
It is desirable for its own ends. Western societies
have inherited much of this ideal unquestioningly and
it has passed unnoticed and relatively unchallenged
into our language. Third World countries at this junc-
ture of their history, now question this word and find
that it shares with Alice in Wonderland, the common
association of most words which mean "what I say they
must mean."

Second, to admit that there is no such thing as
objectivity, is to place the news industry into a
dither, to rob it of its validity and to cause it to
lose the very foundations upon which it rests. Indeed,
to question the valid assumptions upon which the news
industry rests, threatens it with all the insecurity
of incomplete philosophy and a psychology of mind
disastrous for the continuation of its work.

Third, objectivity is a working hypothesis, which
allows most journalists to function and which supports
unconscious shortcomings, and disguises their own very
understandable biases. The most conspicuous error can
then be accommodated on the altar of objectivity. This
is not to imply that journalists look for excuses to
support their errors, but they can operate with the
certainty that there is a built-in system, to which
they can look for comfort when there are errors.

Fourth, objectivity disarms criticism. A journalist who has built up a reputation for objectivity

blunts the sharp end of criticism. A conditioned public takes him more seriously than the journalist who does not try to be objective, or one who colors his prose with subjective references.

Fifth, objectivity allows the journalist to presume that the reader believes he is trying to present an accurate picture of the story, relatively free from biases, when this might be most untrue. All stories are biased and written from the perspective of the writer, whose perceptions are influenced by his value judgement and that of the society of which he is a part.

Thus, the myth of objectivity persists because there are powerful reasons why it should. No less than the philosophical foundation of Western society is involved. No country will surrender this myth willingly, and since it is unable to do so, builds up powerful reasons for it to persist. Any attempts to violate the myth is heavily criticized, for it is the moral and righteous arm of a hard-nosed, ruthless profession. It persists especially in Western dealings with the Third World. The Third World, relatively new, an uncertain force, possibilities undefined is the object of suspicion. It is precisely because it has dared to challenge the old, that the reaction and responses of the Western world have been so sensitive. When critics excoriate the press of the Third World for being "non-free", they do not consider that its press has not known "freedom"; and certainly in the case of some African countries, expatriates and their media showed an overwhelming degree of hostility to the independence movements. 1/ Therefore, a free press was an institution devoutly to be wished and which was conspicuous by its absence.

The press was related to colonial survival, which it did everything to enhance. It was not by any means a training ground for the libertarian ideal, which many in the West now wish to see. In fact, some of the same elements, which now most lament the passing of the free press, are those in earlier times which did everything to stifle its birth, and to ensure its demise where it precariously existed. Now, with all the moral fervor which distance and false rectitude can summon, they take up the crusade against those countries that do not fit the "nice" definition of a free press, whose growth for the most part, they did everything to discourage.

But even if objectivity were possible, it is doubted whether the journalist is capable of attaining it, within his own country, or outside of it. Too many hidden and obvious variables such as class, color, religion, to name a few, divide and perplex his intelligence, making him a prey to an all too hidden bias.

The predilection of a journalist brought up in the city, schooled at an Ivy League University, a graduate degree in journalism from Columbia, a stint at the New York Times or the Associated Press, and an extended assignment in a foreign country (say) Vietnam at the height of the American involvement, becomes understandable. This same young person must rid himself/herself of cultural myopia before bringing to the report the attributes of his craft.

The reference to military conflict is deliberate, for it is at a time like this that the demands of speed, accuracy, reflection, and intelligence come together or should. Yet it is precisely at such times that journalists are apt to fail, or to put it charitably, successes and failures are more readily noticed. (The inability of the New York Times editorial staff to fully understand the implications of the Cold War period is recorded by James Aronson 2/; and David Halberstam mocked the intelligentsia, including journalists, for failure to fully report the Vietnam war. 3/ Full disclosure can at times cause embarrassment; and the revelation of the bombing of Cambodia and the reactions of the former U.S. Secretary of State, Henry Kissinger, provide good copy.)

Failure is often not due to lack of intelligence, which really means the inability to grasp the story behind the facts, but is often a result of intercultural forces, which are a deep divide, and difficult to bridge. There is nothing in past experience to assist. Few journalists are capable of transcending the past easily, quickly and gracefully; and why should they, there is no obvious reward for so doing. The home market for news from the Third World is confined largely to metropolitan readers whose interests need occasionally to be quickened by the sensationalism of a coup d'etat, massacre, or national disaster. Besides, these journalists would agree that goodwill in international relations are ephemeral commodities, which yield no ready dividend. And the journalist sent out from New York City to Nairobi, for example, is anxious to return to headquarters, for well he knows that the longer he stays abroad, the more difficult it can be to return, and in sight and sound of those who would promote him. Hence his sojourn abroad, while profitable in broadening experience and sharpening skills, is a period of gestation, spent in waiting for the rewards of return. This period can be all the more aggravating to magazine correspondents, whose copy is rewritten and there is not even the satisfaction of seeing what one has written printed.

The journalist abroad must bear three important burdens with him: what is news for the home market; what he himself perceives as news; and what the society he represents consider as news. And like a court jester, he must carefully balance the claims of the three. In the first case, what is news for the home market is not often clear. Good copy depends on who reads it and the "sense" in which it is read, and there is no unanimity. In fact, research suggests that a variety of factors influence the perception of what is news. 5/ 6/ 7/

News, runs a saying, which may be apocryphal, is like food, it is the preparation which makes it exciting; and enormous differences exist between the French, English and Soviet preparations. An individual editor, like a chef at work, selectively perceives elements of a good story and goes about the task with an eye to what the home reader wants. His perception is based as much on his "news sense" as on prior experience of similar such news events. The final copy is therefore a collage, his perception of what news is, and an understanding of the readership. The crucial element, which can be omitted is the "value" of the news which comes from abroad, or the fidelity of the source.

News is not a stationary commodity, gathered in one place and sent to another. It is a value system which belongs to source as well as to the person who gathers it, which incorporates them both. That value system is part of the network of intercultural and interpersonal communication variables, which affect the gathering, selection and publication of it, quite apart from political and social systems, which demand additional considerations.

News for the home market is subject to the translation of values from one culture to another. This is

57

difficult at the best of times, troublesome under usual conditions and impossible under conditions of crisis. The action-oriented press of the West (excluding, perhaps, those of countries that had colonies, for they are in a better position to exercise judgement because of this special relationship, even though they sometimes do not), is more often concerned with events, occurrences and hard news, than with examination of the issues. This view is prevalent, when the news occurs in countries of no immediate strategic or economic importance. The eccentricities of former President Bokassa of the Central African Republic and the brutalities of former President Amin of Uganda, are of less importance to the New York Times than the dictatorship of Somoza of Nicaragua, because Nicaragua is of greater strategic importance to the U.S. than either the Central African Republic, or Uganda. Accordingly, news copy of Nicaragua will be more analytical than that concerning either of the two African countries.

It is wise too to emphasize that a newspaper is an index of the society it serves and an editor who decides how to treat a particular story usually has a fair basis for so doing. Sophisticated media research organizations keep a steady pulse on public attitudes and the editor is attuned to the public interest. Judgement is therefore based apparently on sound evidence.

The journalist abroad is not in this certain position. His perspective on what is news is influenced by the field in which he finds himself and his attitudes often undergo substantial and often radical change. A typical network editor who has been exposed to the ways of the establishment, can find it difficult to operate in a multi-ethnic environment. 7/ What he perceives as news abroad, therefore, can be a sharp departure from that considered news at home. His own conditioning changes because he is exposed to a new environment, which becomes the stage for a conflict of values.

One view holds that the professional journalist brings to his craft a professionalism and expertise regardless of the situation. This view is a limited one and omits the influence of environmental factors, character and other circumstance on human conduct. It is idealistic and does not square with realities. The exercise of a craft or skill is as much the subject of professional discipline as is interpretation and the latter is subject to the tempers and tantrums of bureau chiefs, producers, foreign editors, managing editors and the hazards of fortune.

Hence, because of a possible conflict of values and also a change in values, the journalist abroad perceives the news in a way that may be substantially different to what he is accustomed. Of greatest importance is his exposure to the change within the country he is based. Sources of information are often influenced by the kinds of questions asked and are less valuable than (say) similar sources in Western countries. The Hawthorne effect, first noticed in a factory where workers gave responses to questions put to them on the basis of what they believed would please the questioner, becomes a factor. This effect is prevalent in those countries not accustomed to the cut and thrust of modern urban journalism.

As efficacious as these methods are in Western societies, they sometimes find little sympathy outside these circles. What is news does not travel well and there is no universal validity about its definition. Cultures understand and treat news and the news process differently and generally in keeping with cultural heritage. The journalists abroad must seek to know the cultural roots of the country before he can function in a manner conversant with his profession. 8/ If he fails to do this he will discover the difficulty of reporting from a foreign country is compounded by his ignorance of it. Difficulty breeds frustration and his copy will reflect his aggravation. One writer enumerates eight factors which contribute to a gap in communication between Western countries and Africa, but they might equally apply to Third World countries on the whole. 9/

1.   Lack of conceptual tools for
     grasping political events

The foreign correspondent is a creature of relatively recent vintage. Patrick Kingsley reports glowingly of this breed of once hardy men who covered the war in the Crimea in the nineteenth century and who were inseparable from the soldiers in the battlefield, often covering stories at great personal danger and risk. 10/ They would disappear under cover of darkness to send their stories to headquarters. The Second World War had its own fleet of correspondents following the several armies across Europe; and an Edward

R. Murrow, William Shriver and the Australian Chester
Wilmot became famous for their graphic recreation of
an ambience. But the Second World War arguably saw
the last of this breed of journalist who could write
under conditions of stress and hardship without sacrifice to the canons of the trade; namely, the pursuit
of objectivity, accuracy and sensitivity.

        The foreign correspondent today is unlike that,
not because he necessarily lacks the qualities of those
mentioned, but because the conditions for their exercise are different. The speed with which modern technology enables messages to travel, has brought about
objective changes for the practice of the profession.

        For example, the demands for speed hasten the
gathering and the transmission of news. The court-
ship of a reading public by competitive news media
shapes the news process. With the rise in the television audience, there is great pressure on the newspapers and the periodicals to bring out and produce
new material. A reading audience, conditioned to the
changing visualization of television, grows impatient
with newspapers, which do not stimulate the fancy for
the new and the sensational. News is that which sells.

        The foreign correspondent is a part of that
decline. He generally represents a newspaper which
cannot--assuming it were willing--devote much space
to foreign news. His available space is limited to
begin with and what he has to say must be compressed
within set boundaries, which may be broken for the sensational alone, e.g., the Jonestown affair or the fall
of Amin (see Appendix II). Limitations of space affects
other avenues of coverage. There is in consequence
less interest in the specialist who can provide searching analysis and more on the generalist, who can piece
together stories for general distribution. In the
matter of deadlines, shrinking space and competition
for the advertising dollar, the journalist learns to
parlay words. He learns to separate news from analysis; in television reporting he learns to join news
and commentary if and when they both relate, to spicen
a story. Thus a kind of agreeable subjectivity replaces the analysis of a condition, often a critical
condition, affecting a particular country. For example, the New York Times analysis of Jamaica.

        "For almost two weeks the tropical rains
    washed over this lush mountainous island.

60

The downpour deepened potholes in the streets
of Kingston that could swallow a car, swept
away bridges and roads and wiped out a fifth
of the sugar crop.

"The debris magnifies the disrepair of this
impoverished capital, a prototype of one of
the deteriorating third-world cities described in the grim prose of the Caribbean
novelist V. J. Naipaul." 11/

Witness how quickly the scene is set and the cruel
elements which affect a decaying city become a symbol
of all the decaying cities of the Third World. But as
we know, cities decay for reasons which have nothing
to do with poverty. There are rich cities which are
in decay. New York City boasts a population of 10
million and is a decaying city for other reasons: 12/
the growth of the suburb and the city's diminished
tax base, inflation and the urban poor who fight a
losing battle against it; racial discrimination; institutional racism which stalls the ambitions of those
who have begun to climb the ladder; and the difficult
if not impossible road to upward mobility by those who
come from the bottom of the social scale. 13/

Cities deteriorate for reasons other than those
advanced for a Kingston in decay. A more searching
analysis would denote that cities in general and third
world cities in particular tend to house large accumu-
lations of people, living together in an atmosphere
of hurly-burly that is both stimulating and real.
Much of the problems of cities results from the pressure on social services by sheer numbers. But cities
do not decay from poverty. They decay when people
decide to leave them, when they become uninhabitable,
when they lose the magic, which caused them to be what
they are, and social emptiness becomes the pastime of
deserted streets and worn out buildings. Then a city
can be said to have decayed. No one who has seen the
city of Calcutta, with its teeming millions and its
exhausted social services, its street beggars and its
filth, would call it a decaying city. On the contrary,
Calcutta is an active city and bustling, which during
the day forgets its problems and strives in occupation
and human contact to come to grips with its essence,
which is survival. Writers like V.S. Naipaul who
portray the reality of a "Civilization Wounded" and
"An Area of Darkness," see problems and not people and

forget the human resources, which are themselves part
of the solution to problems. 14/

Increasingly also, political problems become per-
sonalized, probably because writers lack the skill for
analysis of the problems, which are part of this political analysis. Also, television in its highly personal
manner has converted an objective reality into a personal one. Thus, in our time the power of the U.S.
Congress has quite paled beside the prestige of the
Presidency; and personal diplomacy is of greater significance than the more painstaking efforts behind
national consensus. A Prime Minister personalizes a
whole country, in much the same way as a President
symbolizes another, and the elected representatives of
the people, have become of decreasing importance,
figuratively as well as metaphorically.

"For example, the man in the eye of the hur-
ricane is Prime Minister Michael N. Manley.
Tall, lean, strikingly handsome at the age
of 55, he is one of the most charismatic
leaders in the developing world, rivaled by
only his close friend Fidel Castro. At the
recent conference of third-world nations in
Havana, Mr. Manley demonstrated his global
stature by leading the fight to get the oil
producers to agree to discuss special relief for the developing countries, a break-
through that could bring enormous benefits
to the world's poor. Yet in Jamaica this
glamorous son of an English artist and of
the first Prime Minister of Jamaica is
rapidly losing support." 15/

The visual picture is strong and a substitute for
the television picture that would confirm Mr. Manley's
handsomeness, qualities of leadership and stature.
His impeccable forbears--a distinguished father and an
English mother, place him within an out-of-date English
class system, and much of what follows, locates Manley
and his contradictions at the center of Jamaica's political life, making him responsible for its tone.

"On the surface Mr. Manley is a man who
lives on a salary of $12,000, drives a
small Fiat, runs three miles a day, plays
tennis and neither drinks nor smokes. In
keeping with a sense of theater, and with

62

a theory that postcolonial societies should
spurn inappropriate Western dress, he wears
a carefully tailored kareba, a suit in bush-
jacket style. His gardens in the hills beyond Kingston produce "the best roses in
Jamaica." His son is studying economics in
Havana; his wife, his fourth, is writing a
thesis on psychological barriers to development; his father, Norman, is buried in
National Heroes Circle." 16/

The rest of the article is a search for the meaning to Mr. Manley's apparent "contradictions," his
goal of democratic socialism, the economic slump
brought about by the rigidity of the conditions set by
the International Monetary Fund, the flight of the middle classes, and Manley's efforts to bolster Jamaica.
But the personalizing of Manley sticks out beyond the
inadequate attempt to analyze the Jamaican situation.

Trivializing the content of the meaningful is the
direction of journalism, which must balance words and
space, against advertising revenues, a readership conditioned to a narrow attention span and the substantial demands of news from a demanding world. The personalizing of a national leader, whoever he may be,
distorts the reality of news and the news process, by
omitting other considerations which might not be shaped
by the leader at all.

Politics in the Third World demands an understanding of a complex web of human relationships, which can
involve national divisions of race, religion, to a
bewildering degree. These elements also occupy Western countries, but the crucial difference is that the
latter are established and have gone through their
developmental problems, even though some problems like
the urban-rural dichotomy remain to haunt. Third
World countries, on the other hand, are in the throes
of development, often accompanied by social tension as
policies, programs and information plot their way
through the social fabric of the nation.

2.   Popular prejudice

The lack or absence of conceptual tools with
which to evaluate events renders the foreign correspondent insecure. He is personally vulnerable because,
without the tools to evaluate, he is unable to do his

63

job well. His reports are daily scrutinized by his colleagues at home and by the ministries within the host country which observe his work, and well he knows that he can only remain in the country if he enjoys the support of the authorities; and indeed, he may find that his sources of information dry up, which is often an indirect signal that he no longer is welcome. But there are ways of circumventing this lack of conceptual tools.

One way is time-honored. Close relations are established among visiting journalists who frequent a popular hotel or who congregate at the noon hour at a bar and exchange information. 17/ The more seasoned journalists have pride of place and hold court to the more recent arrivals.

Another is to seek expatriates, selecting those either on the basis of views sympathetic to the regime, or antagonistic to it, or frequently both. The report then represents a "mix" of opinions, balancing the one side against the other and in this way, objectivity is presumed. This largely explains the staid similarity of many of the news reports from Third World countries, sensation notwithstanding.

The two mentioned ways in which foreign correspondents avoid the painful admission of their own ignorance, in the face of complex situations and seek help, presume that they are interested in discerning and finding out facts or lack of them, (for often there are no facts to report and one is left to make them up--a position all too frequent). But there are cases where reporters are not interested in this and treat the business of facts and the gathering of them as a troublesome inconvenience: first, where the reporter is briefed about what he is to report and which side to support. The second case involves war coverage, where the reporter has to substantiate a given position and writes with that in mind. This is particularly so when correspondents represent national press systems which are under the control of the government. They are expected to maintain fixed positions as they go through the ritual of interpreting the news in keeping with national objectives, e.g., the work of the Soviet news agency, Tass.

News agencies suffer from the objective fallacy. They serve an audience already conditioned as to what it wants. They must cater to that audience or lose credibility. A commercial press cannot purely reflect audience interests, but must inevitably serve the interests of advertisers. This is not to impute unfair motives to the news managers, but only to admit that the ownership of the news media carries with it obligations which are inseparable from news values.

One of these obligations is to perpetuate the image of dependency and despair among the peoples of the Third World, who powerless to change circumstance, await the coming of assistance from the industrialized countries. It therefore becomes most difficult for a correspondent, reporting from (say) Bolivia, on the expansion of a tin mine, not to include at least a passing reference to the plight of management in the face of lazy Indians. Equally, it is also difficult to write from almost any country in Africa, without referring to the many problems that continent faces. A hint at the solutions or the efforts at finding solutions, especially those independent of external aid, is never good copy. News fulfills and satisfies the need for a dependent psychology, which in turn creates its own dependency.

Dependent relationships reinforce certain powerful institutions: the Established Church, for instance. The notion of a universal God, white in color, benign, counselling obedience, and submission, adherence to the status quo, opposed to birth control, is an image often at odds with the more demanding concerns of national development. Acquiescence to a present structure as a preparation for life to come, is not the most vigorous policy for changing the harsh conditions of daily life. A person who believes that the best life is yet to come, is likely to abide the inadequacies of the present without doing much to change them.

Two views are significant: the first has to do with the maintenance of the belief that the Third World is the happy hunting ground for the expansion of the Church--a view held by church leaders from a variety of denominations; the second view supports the first; that is, the belief that they are themselves the instruments of this noble work.

The Church is discussed because it illustrates how an institution can and does extend its influence into other countries, armed with ideologies which may be inimical to development and how, very often, these

65

ideologies are defended both by their own countries and those in which they crusade. Nevertheless, the more humanitarian aspects of church work deserve commendation.

The Church is not the only institution which seeks a continued foothold in the Third World. Transnational corporations also perform similar tasks; and it can be argued that while the transnational corporation is in the business of making men greedy and greedy men more greedy, the Church is in the business of saving the souls of the greedy. Both institutions work unwittingly together and an alliance of the two can be a formidable phalanx; indeed the Church of England is still held to be the Tory party at prayer.

The psyche of portions of the Third World is involved in these institutional arrangements. Thus, an informal alliance can exist between Church, State and Corporation, by which each respects the other's work and appropriate domain, though not deliberately. But the State is quick to come to the aid of the Church, if and when events deem this necessary. Belgium intervention in the Congo crisis was said to have been due to the slaughter of a few Roman Catholic nuns in Stanleyville, and the death of Dr. Paul Carlson, the American missionary. Ronald Segal, discussing the Time magazine report, December 4, 1964, complained that the magazine provided less than fair coverage and ignored the atrocities perpetuated by white mercenaries against Africans, and the many Africans who died to save white lives against the continual background of racial pain in Africa. 18/

Thus the Third World is a continued victim of popular prejudice, which defines its expectations in terms of casual and careless standards, serving appointed beliefs and attitudes. Nowhere is this reflected more than in the dramatic presentation of news.

Drama as news value. It is an ill wind which blows nothing of news value from a Third World country, except "dramatic" news. By dramatic, we mean the capacity of news to move the emotions. Thus a news event with this specific quality becomes theater, with the particular cathartic quality of the theater, purging the emotions of feelings. But drama is not always meant to be cathartic. It can stun, excite,

66

stimulate and compel and transferred to a news event makes it gripping. News from the Third World needs the dramatic "feel" in order to merit a place in the columns of most newspapers and certainly in the visual presentation in television stations. Why is this?

Again, hidden interpersonal and intercultural forces are at work. The reporter often produces work, which he believes is part of "official" newspaper or network policy. Thus he is a victim of forces which he cannot control or seldom influence. "Americans have an isolationist tendency to imagine all events occur within their borders," says Robin Winks, professor of history at Yale University, 19/ an insularity which is not confined to news events. Because of this, news from the rest of the world can only compete on the domestic market if it is seen in a different light. To displace the morning round and daily diet of local offerings, news from foreign sources must be outstanding indeed. Nothing but the exceptional will replace the metropolitan news in provincial newspapers. News has inherited that quality of instantaneousness from television and some of its excitement. A palace coup in Morocco, where power changes hands with minimal loss of blood is of limited news value. But a coup d'etat in Gabon, for instance, where after much fighting in the streets, a rival takes over the government, imposes martial law, proceeds to exact terrible vengeance on his enemies through executions, public torture and all the assorted accoutrements which accompany such things, this is more than a diversion. It is a dramatic occurrence, with which the reader can identify. Make these events run over a week or so, for a battery of television cameras and newspaper reporters to add color with on-the-spot details and what results is stunningly dramatic.

News selection is not by happenstance, vagary, or interpretation. One researcher reveals that at one television network a Racial Equivalence Scale guides the efforts of journalists. The Scale shows the minimum number of people who must die in airplane crashes in different countries before the crash becomes newsworthy. As one writer pointed out "one hundred Czechs were equal to forty-three Frenchmen and the Paraguayans were at the bottom." 20/ This standard is by no means confined to the American landscape. 21/

Similar also, is the preoccupation with the individual, often at the expense of the societies of

which they are a part. This individualistic approach
frowns on group identification as potentially destructive of independence, the bedrock of the Protestant
ethic. This independent spirit must be guarded against
contamination with group causes, which can lead to conformity, a dulling of initiative, and a decline in
productive capacity. The relationship between personal independence and productive capacity on the one
hand, and group identification, loss of independence,
the substitution of public ownership for private ownership on the other, largely, though not completely,
explains the suspicion if not antipathy with which
socialism is viewed in Western society. The fixation
with the individual personality explains why it is difficult for the media to understand the widespread significance of group causes. The media, therefore, in
their own appointed manner, search for and recognize
a leader of a group, who will be courted and then
having exhausted its attention, drop him just as quickly and easily as they found him.

Giving credibility to a leader is the surest means
of destroying a movement and the leader. 22/ There are
of course exceptions. The Civil Rights Movement became
an important story in the 1960s, because of and indeed
in spite of Martin Luther King, who was not created
by the mass media, but existed in spite of them. The
movement was significant to American society and its
deliberations and demonstrations were carefully and
faithfully recorded. Once this challenged faded and
the movement declined as a major news story after Dr.
King's death, there was little need for the media to
deal with inequity and social justice. 23/

That the media do not must be attributed to both
thelack of focus of the movement (though not lack of
ambition), and the decline of social disorder which it
once threatened. The return of this threat would
quickly change the existing affairs and the media would
hastily seek and find a responsible leader on whom to
focus attention. 24/ Mass media identification of a
leader and all that entails is the reason why many
groups prefer to diffuse. They attract less attention,
but share among themselves a unity and a purpose, which
comes from addiction to a common cause.

Another noteworthy feature also is the group without recognizeable leadership is not taken seriously by
the mass media because neither praise nor blame can be
attached to it; an essential quality which makes it

newsworthy is missing. It is for this reason that deviant or dissident groups must occasionally bestir themselves in public, or lose claim as serious news contenders; and groups without leadership are in danger of losing their credibility altogether. The Klu Klux Klan finds it necessary to stir up demonstrations under the guise of membership drives, but in reality the group is keeping its image before the news peddlers, reminding them that they are by no means a spent force. Groups without apparent leadership are in constant danger of losing credibility, for the mass media do not expose the issues before the public. The absence of an image is equivalent to an image which does not exist. Justice and equality are not newsworthy features and have but marginal if any dramatic value. Violence and demonstration have strong dramatic values.

While leadership of a group in the news ensures some coverage, it does not ensure that the coverage will be adequate. For example, a dictator who is brutal and ruthlessly puts down an insurrection is more likely to get his due deserts in the press than a dictator of the benevolent kind. Amin of Uganda was heaven-sent for Western media. An enormous man, he was a cruel buffoon, whose years as ruler of Uganda was accompanied by every possible violation of civil rights. In addition, he confirmed the worse fears among those who had long suspected, ever since the Congo crisis, that Black Africa was not ready for self-government and therefore should not have been given it in the first place. Such a man could always be depended on for good copy. The Daily Mirror, a London newspaper, at the height of the Amin power, ran a banner: "He's mad." Coverage of the Amin years was always extensive, largely because Amin understood the media's need for sensation.

On the other hand, dictators of a kind who have varied their extravagance, have not been as ready preys for the media, especially those who have been kindly disposed to the U.S. It would make an interesting study to consider dictators for whom law and order have been central to their domestic policy and who have received help from the U.S. The names of Somoza and Trujillo, both assassinated, come to mind. Black Americans have suggested that dictators who are black have been more objects of scorn by the media than those who are non-black.

But drama is not confined to the ranks of excess-
es of dictators. Disasters such as floods, earth-
quakes, other natural hazards are also components of
live theater, which compose the mass media. Unwittingly, mass media in industrialized countries reveal the
somber side of poverty and suffering, which are com-
forting to their sense of security and affluence,
thereby conforming the stereotypic images for which
Third World countries are known. But while the mass
media enhance coverage of disasters, they often do so
at the expense of the necessary "contextual detail",
which would explain all aspects of the story. In fact,
this lack of detail may be one of the niceties of good
television drama, where the unravelling of a story is
kept to its barest essentials, free from complication
or useless narrative. The threadbare storyline is one
of the fundamentals of television outside of the
documentary, which enjoys the luxury of extensive and
searching enquiry and analysis. The mass media
audience thus grows accustomed to and depends on the
simplistic treatment of important issues. The conspicuous lack of background in most stories involving the
Third World is not only seen in television--mentioned
because it is an obvious target and because it has such
an enormous capacity for influencing the public--but in
the other media as well. (It should be pointed out that
the influence of television is not simply restricted to
those who have sets; the television environment is all
around us and television has largely succeeded in
changing the format of newspapers as well as radio.25/)

3.   Substance and the lack of it

     There is an alarming lack of substance in cover-
age of Third World issues. Some would argue that there
is a lack of substance in covering most issues, whether
domestic or foreign, and certainly it is true to say
that domestic concerns influence those that are foreign.
For example, the shortage of gasoline in the U.S. during
the summer of 1979 influenced the coverage of the Middle
East situation and the resignation of Andrew Young, U.S.
Ambassador to the United Nations, triggered renewed interest in the relations between the Arab world, Israel
and the U.S.

     There is reason for this lack of coverage. First,
the Third World in general must compete with news from
Europe and the U.S., which are the centers of the industrial world and occupy "most favored" continent

status. This competition is unequal, for they share
strong ties, strengthened by corporate interests, technology and advanced nuclear engineering. Also, ownership of news agencies carries with it important and
significant prestige. These function as "gatekeepers"
which can control the flow of news and monitor the
news. It is easy to see their value as organs which
"process" the news. This occurs in radio, which relies
on news prepared specially for radio by the Associated
Press and UPI and sent by teleprinter to radio stations.
Because the news is already "processed" and therefore
ready for broadcast, it is known as "rip and read"
copy.

The processing of news is in keeping with the news
agency function as power broker. Prestige makes it
part of the power structure; for example, the Associated Press is a private news agency formed by an amal-
gamation of newspapers. It can hardly be argued that
the Associated Press and any other national news agency
does not wield immense influence. And not to be aware
of the subtle pressures which exist in a conventional
democracy is to bury one's head in the sand. 26/

Indeed, the five top news agencies are owned by
four nations and this, together with the giant technological productive capacity of these nations, make
them virtual leaders in the field of information processing. A large concentration of population among
these countries and the development of a vast array
of social services as well as wealth, stimulates information services and in turn global information patterns.

A number of factors influence global information
flow and chief among these are politics, economics
and compelling nuclear capability. Countries strong
in these capacities dominate the news and also ensure
that it flows in one direction only--from the rich
industrial nations to the developing ones. In fact,
the one way flow of information guarantees that events
of importance in the industrialized countries is immediately communicated to the developing world.

News flow from the industrialized countries is
substantial compared to that within the Third World
and it is also unbalanced. The bias towards the industrialized countries, created by conditions which
promote the gathering and dissemination of news, is

therefore responsible for at least some distortion of
news and values.

But the flow of news must not be considered as
the only area of contention. News is part of the
general flow of informational materials between countries, including books, radio and television sets,
films and educational materials. The argument against
unrestricted entry of these products is two-fold:
first, that restriction protects local industry and
raises revenue through taxation and second, that unrestricted entry of cultural artefacts disturbs the
delicate balance of the national culture industry.
The first argument is understandable: Revenue gained
from restriction is relatively small (presuming that
we are dealing with countries which have a one-crop
economy, usually an agriculture crop and minimal industrial potential); and a case can be made out for
loosening too tight controls on the importation of
goods and services from abroad. This consideration
assumes tremendous importance in the light of depleted
foreign exchange and a government would often consider
as priorities industrial and military equipment over
books and informational supplies.

The restriction on the flow of information, for
whatever reasons advanced, serves to underline the differences between the industrial countries and the Third
World. The complaints of the latter are an echo and a
refinement of the total world economic situation, which
enrich those who already have and impoverish those who
are already poor.

But riches and poverty do not completely explain
substance or the lack of it. A definition of what is
news is more to the point. Here basic differences appear. Industrialized countries see the function of
news as essentially informing as opposed to influencing,
which is the purpose of propaganda. But the process of
informing is a double-edged sword, for it carries with
it the implication of both influence and propaganda.

These ideas--and a definition is a precise idea--
about what constitutes news are by no means universal,
nor do they carry universal applicability. News may be
culture-specific: and what is news in one society may
not be news in another. News is a melange which includes ideas, attitudes and beliefs and the events to
which these relate as well as to the cultural milieu.
But news is also ideological and serves the beliefs

72

and governing ideology of particular countries.

Thus the Western industrialized countries which espouse capitalism support a highly competitive news system, where news is a commodity bought by the consumer. The consumer must therefore be kept "happy" with a continuous bombardment of news which, in its sensationalism and flamboyance, equals the consumer's own expectations. Thus, news is crisis-oriented.

Vietnam was the first major conflict that engaged television and it had limited dramatic potential and some excitement. Painted early in its history as an American war against communism, it never succeeded until the Tet offensive in rising above a purely local situation, which was troublesome, but which would eventually be taken care of. Then the view that it was somehow an official war, conducted and orchestrated from Washington, gained currency. Official sources stage-managed the war by the skilful use of propaganda, which is the management of news for a particular purpose. 28/ The mass media went along with the administration's version of the war, substituting dramatic coverage for substantive reporting. The audience, daily fed by pictures from the battlefield, came to expect them as routine, and advertisers and sponsors ever watchful for public trends, followed the general direction resignedly.

Thus, crisis-orientation tends to exclude substance and is often at the expense of it. The mass media in America follow the largest number principle; to put it bluntly, it goes after large audiences, for it is through these that commercial profits are assured. Stories which appeal to the swelling multitude, irrespective of content or value, are treated with all the gusto of a religious rite. When these stories have national appeal, they are generously covered. International news is a thinly veiled concern depending and dependent on the importance of the event, the value judgement of an editor, or the philosophical exercises of a producer, who might reason that the audience ought to know what is in its interests, or indeed what its own best interests are.

Substance in the news is also determined by other considerations: the vagaries of the human condition, disguised to look like intellectual or public affairs concerns. American foreign policy interests and priorities always make good copy and news organizations follow that rough guideline. They know that the American people can be treated for purposes of foreign news as one unit and it is just as easy to follow the lead of the State Department as the dictates of journalism. There is little need to deviate from the official line, in so far as foreign news is concerned. 29/

4. News as a factor of time

Lack of substance in reporting the Third World is only equalled by the swiftness with which interest in its news declines. To a great extent news is always time-conscious and no one would wish to deny that it should be so; in fact, the commercial constraints under which news works make it imperative that time considerations be kept in the foreground. The need to make a profit is often associated with the need to change and the more immediate the change the corresponding loss in attention span and the loss of interest. Topic interest decreases and with it the value of news. The decline in news value as a result of market forces, ensures that a story is not completely covered, or dropped before a reliable picture of it is presented to the audience.

The economic factor plays havoc with Third World news. Already scarce, limited to an audience only marginally interested at the best of times, it suffers from inadequate coverage because nothing has been done to induce substantial coverage, or promote demand for it. The reasons are not completely clear. Journalists do not often consider the public they write for, beyond making copy readable and simple and accurate. In a large country social differentiation by race, class, religion and occupation makes it difficult for the journalist to bear in mind the needs of a specific readership. Production considerations emphasize brevity, terseness and efficiency in the use of space.

The tragedy of the Third World is that its news does not fit into the cultural perspectives of the West and because of it, treatment outside of crisis situations, is subjected to certain limitations. Cultural myopia explains the poverty of archives and research material.

5. Poverty of research material

This is by no means confined to newspaper morgues; national and university libraries are hardly better off. When Black Studies programs became interested in the African diaspora, the lack of books and related educational material in general circulation was discouraging. The Third World is still considered as refinery for university tastes and outside of crisis news, is not the proper concern of journalists. Universities, happy to find themselves in the unexpected position of national reverence, respond by attempting to accommodate the vacuum. International programs embracing all aspects of the Third World, are a popular part of the offerings of most graduate schools and, together with the modern popularity of communication studies, make certain of at least a semblance of respectability in library stocks. Occasionally, there is a marriage of interests, when the university opens its doors to the select few journalists, but the practice is not widespread, a trickle rather than a flow.30/

The lack of material and archives indicates an intellectual arrogance, which is inseparable from national conceit. The attitude seems to be "this is not properly within our sphere of interest and in any case, we know all about it." The installation of computer and data banks has increased information storage capabilities of the news agencies, which can immediately obtain the necessary background information. 31/ But given this facility, it is still a far cry from getting a newspaper editor to utilize background material on a continuing basis, given the gravity of a story; or, for that matter, to get a producer to give any but superficial treatment of a burning issue.

The truth is that each news story is very much the end result of a chain of events, particularly if that event has political undertones. Since the news from the Third World is crisis news, demanding immediate treatment, there is little tendency to discuss the background to the chain of events, except at the level of the national daily, or if that event is of overwhelming significance, a television network might do a documentary.

Jonestown became an international story for the rather obvious reason that it was the largest recorded suicide in history. That alone would not have sufficed to keep it on the front pages of most national

dailies in the U.S., had it not been for the fact that
the suicides were American citizens, who had exported
part of twentieth century America to a Third World
country. Reporters hurriedly brushed up on their geo-
graphy and political science and with a lackadaisical
attention to accuracy, wrote copy embarrassingly short
of their own professed standards (see Appendix III).

It may be argued that circumstances in the Third
World change altogether too rapidly and upset routine
calculations. But the response here is that unless
monitoring of the Third World is institutionalized,
there can be no means for following the likely crisis,
when it erupts. The U.S. State Department manages to
monitor the potential trouble spots around the world,
but there is not always convincing evidence that information assembled in this way does eventually come
out in reasoned and appropriate policy. 32/

News agencies disseminate required background information. But inadequate coverage often lies at the
level of the provincial, small town newspaper, which
does not perceive its interests as consonant with the
world outside. Indeed, this restricted vision of the
world is reinforced by the national obsession with the
greatness of the society and ethnocentrism, which
blinds all but supportive images. Modern American
ethnocentrism is a more aggressive form of jingoism,
which afflicted England in the nineteenth century:
"we've got the ships, we've got the men and we've got
the money too."

This distorted sense of national and international greatness exposes the poverty upon which it rests.
Citizens who do not concern themselves with the world
outside, lack the perspective to deal with the world
within, and suddenly react with surprise, when that
which they see without, does not square with that which
they see within. Discrepancy is the heart and soul of
the matter, the difference between public postures and
private attitudes, the "duplicity theme," or the difference between "what public officials say in public
and private." 33/ Applied to information dissemination, it is a distinction made by Walter Lippman between news and truth. "The function of news is to
signalize an event; the function of truth is to bring
to light the hidden facts, to set them in relation
with each other, and to make a picture of reality on
which men can act." 34/ Unless background information attends the discussion of an event, then that

coverage is a disservice. The audience also is impeded
from intelligently participating in reasoned discourse
on a national level. Unless the hidden agenda, which
is often a part of Third World news, is revealed by
painful attention to background, the news will always
remain superficial and devoid of the larger aspects of
meaning. Clearly, in depth coverage should always accompany the single event. But as we indicated the difficulties are enormous and budgetary considerations
loom large. Take television for example.

Budgets for news operations are carefully husband-
ed and short shrift given an extravagant producer. The
accent is on spending only what is necessary for appropriate coverage of the news event. Costly satellite
operations are discouraged and the filmed report
favored. News stories which originate in major cities
like New York, Chicago and Los Angeles, take prefer-
ence over others because the networks have owned and
operated stations there and already established lines
of communication. Were they to report from other cities, lines would have to be rented.

But budgetary considerations alone do not explain
the lack of research material, the poverty of archives
and the non-existence of files on all but a few Third
World countries. The news which comes from the Third
World cannot be easily categorized. It does not fit
into packages. In a world where images are galore,
they are expected to explain reality without the need
to delve further. Thus a famine can be explained as a
situation in which there is a prolonged scarcity of
food. Television will carry a filmed report, showing
people dying of hunger and thirst and the newspapers
will count the dead and list international rescue
teams. A deeper probing of the problems of famine, its
history, its likelihood of occurrence is less often
seen. This may be so for other reasons.

6.   Forces of "good" and "evil"

A cultural bias in editorial comment shows up when
there is conflict in the Third World. 35/ Because of
the need to attract and keep a mass audience, television must bare stories to the bone in order to keep
them simple and short. No unnecessary qualification
or contingency must distress or confuse the ability
of the audience to comprehend. Mass circulation newspapers take a similar approach. The mass media are
less concerned with educating an audience than

entertaining it and in order for entertainment to be thoroughly convincing, the requisite climate must be prepared. Simplicity and an easy division of forces into "good" and "evil" encourage a ready audience.

But news does not restrict itself to such easy and facile generalizations. Conflict is often a complex business, in which both good and evil are present in unequal proportions; and just as drama has within it the juxtaposition of good and evil, the event, be it ever so humble, often has such ingredients. "Good" and "evil" are not always self-evident and conspicuous to the eye of every beholder. As ethical standards they do not have universal applicability and even if they do, distance, and time restrain judgment and give pause.

Vietnam was a case in point. The Vietcong were the "bad" guys and the South Vietnamese the "good" guys. Castro was and still is a "bad" guy. But Somoza of Nicaragua, until his overthrow, was a "good" guy.

To understand this easy classification is to study the influence of the moral standard, which derives from the influence of organized religion in Western societies. Collective virtue consists of the forces of good triumphing over the forces of evil. But the structural conditions of conflict do not lend themselves to such value judgments. Somoza was more than simply a dictator, good or bad. Somoza was a product of a history dating back to the conquistadores, an institution, moreover, which the U.S. actively supported and still supports, i.e., a socially influential elite as the best safeguard against revolution. The bulk of the people remain unrepresented. In such a climate representative government is at best a pretense, at worse, a mockery. Social restlessness and revolution often accompany this caricature of representation, since government represents nobody but itself. Good and evil do not apply before an investigation is made as to which of the contesting parties provides the best guarantees for the good governance of the State and the security of the people. The same standards should apply to all societies. The demands of the marketplace should never be allowed to replace sober assessment. That they do is reason for the following factor.

78

7. Influence of domestic affairs on foreign news

Foreign news is important only as it is relevant, or perceived as such, to American interests. Foreign news derives its validity from its approximation or distance from such American standards as ethnocentrism, altruistic democracy, responsible capitalism, small-town pastoralism, individualism, moderatism, the pre-servation of the social order, and the need for na-tional leadership. 36/

That foreign news is subject to national images is in itself an indictment of those very images, which are like shadows, depending on a fixture for existence. These national images are not always clear-cut. The national paranoia of communism received a serious jolt after detente and the opening of trade with parts of the loosely-held communist empire to trade and com-merce. The visit of ex-President Nixon to Romania and his subsequent visit to the People's Republic of China confused those dominant anti-communist images, which were succeeded by the more wholesome "relevance to our interests."

Foreign news suffers therefore from the disadvan-tage of being processed through domestic myopia. What is relevant is in the nation's interests and the rest is not worth the bother. One of the difficulties about foreign news is that it cannot be effectively measured. In a nation which places much store by quantitative measures, foreign news has no "consti-tuency" outside of the narrow coterie of the elite. That is not to say that the bulk of the people do not read foreign news, or are not alive to its importance, but it is to say that they are not sensitive to its nuances.

The hostages locked inside the American Embassy compound in Iran, and the frenzied activity of the American government to secure their release, strike a responsive chord in the nation at large. The resig-nation of Andrew Young from the ambassorship of the United Nations, stimulated awareness in Middle East Affairs in a way that only the peace treaty signed be-tween Prime Minister Begin of Israel and President Sadat of Egypt did. Only exceptional news events, which border on the spectacular, can arouse the people from a self-imposed lethargy, from which only imminent national disaster or personal tragedy can awaken them. 37/

That this insulation from the outside world persists, despite all the help and assistance by the Federal government, foundations, universities and the mass media generally is remarkable. 38/ The reasons may be traced both to traditional insularity; that is, the natural tendency on the part of immigrants and others to look askance at the countries left behind, and which had not been able to fulfil their expectations. Or, the need to be accepted in the new world, led them to overcompensate by digging such roots, to the exclusion of what exists beyond the Statue of Liberty, even though this at times created an embarrassing ambivalence. Another reason may be that America's success in the two world wars created an overconfidence from which it has never recovered; added to that, the dependence of the rest of the world on its vast economic wealth and resources, at least for a time, did nothing to allay this towering complex. Further, the pulsating genius of a people, creating and advancing technology to wider limits and beyond, creates an illusion--sometimes dangerous--of invincibility. Why then, should this nation concern itself with what happens beyond its seas?

The question is not rhetorical. It is asked by many who believe that splendid isolation ended with the nineteenth century. At all levels there is but token concern for foreign news. The U.S. is made up of over 3,500 counties, each rejoicing in its own busy Main Street, which represents its own spiritual center. The domestic situation, therefore, is a reflection of this parochial beehive, into which foreign news is not readily admitted. Yet race relations do affect the perception of foreign news.

8.   Race and foreign news

The rise of commercial television has been responsible for the glorification of the image of America as a powerful society. The belief in its own power, to be sure, existed prior to the arrival of television, but it was not as widespread, and the image of power was not as reinforced as it is by television. Today, with television set saturation at 97 per cent, the image is guaranteed to reach all homes; and in any case, as previously noted, the absence of a television set in a home does not diminish the importance of the television environment. 39/

The dominant image on commercial and public television is that of the white male, whose presence implies a judgment of value. 40/ His image invokes racial exclusivity and an arbitrary power, which the Federal Communications Commission (FCC) only remotely keeps in check by the merest pretence at regulation. In fact, the FCC, which supposedly operates in the public's interest, honors its legal commitment in a lopsided way. 41/ A clause in the Federal Communications Act of 1934 states that broadcast stations operate in the "public interest, convenience and necessity," a maid-of-all-work provision, which means specifically everything and nothing at one and the same time. Thus, renewal proceedings, when broadcast stations must show how they have served the public, or run the risk of losing their licenses, are almost a formality. 42/ While blame must not be unfairly distributed, the inadequate staff and working conditions of the FCC makes it difficult to investigate every license renewal carefully, given the number of complaints which comes from the irate citizen. Much of the work in civic responsibility is largely due to the vigor of the United Church of Christ, the National Organization for Women, Action for Children's Television and Best Efforts for Soul on Television. 43/

Corporate structures pay lip service to improved race relations, but the task needs a watchfulness and attention often quite beyond the capacity of institutions. This accounts for the situation of the white male. Mass media institutions support, fortify and reinforce this image and the white male can with casual concern for the rights of the non-white, trample upon their interests without much ado. The white image on television bolstered by his ready access to the media in general, is all pervasive and stands as a permanent indictment against American society. The Report of the National Advisory Commission Civil Disorders declared that white society was deeply implicated in the ghetto. But it was the news media which failed to analyze and report adequately on racial problems in the U.S. and as a related matter, to meet the black's related problems in journalism. 44/ A decade later the Village Voice charges the New York Times with racial discrimination, 45/ and the influential black newspaper, the Amsterdam News, accuses the Daily News of the same thing. 46/ Both newspapers seem not to have taken the recommendations of the Report seriously, joining a substantial group nationwide which is guilty of omission at the worst of times and inadequate coverage at the best of times.

Blacks and other non-white minorities have never taken their rightful place in American society, because they have not been allowed to. The three factors responsible are: the disability of race; inability to enter into the political system effectively; and cultural factors. All are inherent in the seeds of an exclusive racism. 47/

But it doesn't end there. A home-grown racism is incapable of seeing the world, except through the prism of race. Foreign news is seen necessarily through the racial perspective, be it ever so distant, be it ever so slight, the "racial angle" would be sought out and revealed in all its brash detail.

An excessive concern for race on the domestic scene has led journalists to interpret incidents of racial activity abroad as a simple variant of the American experience. They lack the cultural perspective to deal with race as more than social and economic injustice. They cannot see race as an adjustment to the political realities, such as cultural nationalism and economic independence on a worldwide scale. They can think of race only within the confines of an outdated physical anthropological and unscientific attribute of color. They could not and still cannot see the race has been circumscribed by the non-white; and the non-aligned movement is demanding a revision of economic and other relations. The result of which is to negate race as a staple in human affairs. It was this that Fanon referred to as the Wretched of the Earth throwing off their chains and defining themselves on their own terms. 48/

The Black American is trying to do precisely that, but because he does not control the economic domain, can make little inroad against racial injustice and political power. The white worker likewise is in the same predicament, but as he is part of the majority, deceives himself that he owns part of the system, which also persecutes him. What he doesn't know, unless he realizes the roots of his own oppression, is that he, too, is powerless to control the forces that have dominion over him. In any event, accustomed as he is to occasional handouts, he supports the very system he should disavow, thereby conspiring in his own debility and oppression. His problem, therefore, is economic justice.

There is a direct connection between racial injustice and economic power and it is in the interests of those with economic power to preserve relations which consolidate and prolong power. One way to preserve power is by means of the systematic application of images, which either negate the existence of, ridicule, or make a caricature of minority culture. These images are no haphazard affair; but are part of a social policy, which may have deliberately been fashioned for dealing with as explosive an issue as race relations.

Monopoly ownership of the mass media dictates both the quality and quantity of the images. Monopoly of this kind raises important questions of public policy and social responsibility. Involved here are power relationships, which have sorely missed, avoided, or neglected black Americans. Where the media have paid any attention, are in those areas, where images conform to their own diagnosis of the racial ethic and the systems of rewards, which the society promises for the faithful.

Mass media institutions and their power structure have relied on three ideological components that have been part of colonial societies. Black Americans are confronted by the ritual of enactment of a system which has had many distinguished forbears: colonialism, exploitation and elitism. 49/

There is no panacea for racial harmony. Black Americans, realizing this, have opted for struggle as a means of maintaining psychic harmony, all but destroyed in the fatigue of battle and conflict and for such limited gains as chance their way from time to time.

Yet there was evidence of the desire to move into other areas, which critically concern the future of black and white people. Dr. Martin Luther King realized the opportunity of Vietnam to remind the nation of its tenuous, precarious moral balance in prosecuting a war, which did not have strong or redeeming

83

moral claims. That the war was fought against non-white people was noticed. The hue and cry at the United Nations against what appeared to be naked aggression, did not fall on deaf ears, just as the earlier French role in Vietnam, did not pass unnoticed. 50/ Racism, therefore, moved out of the domestic arena on to the world stage, embarrassing those countries which actively practiced it, and confusing others, which pretended it did not exist. Andrew Young, the former U.S. representative to the United Nations, in a speech to black clergy, urged them to be concerned with the Palestinian issue in the Middle East, for it was directly related to the well-being of black Americans. 51/

The internationalizing of the race issue is an acknowledgement that power relationships have gone beyond the domestic scene. It is also both a confession and a failure: namely, that efforts to bring about social and economic justice have failed, and there is need for additional input from outside to restore reason and sanity.

Unfortunately, sanity is not evident. The universal condemnation by the U.S. press of the Popular Unity government of Chile is a case in point. The generalized drivel, which recorded the attempts by the legal government of President Allende to conduct affairs, was recorded everywhere. In similar vein reporting Castro's Cuba and Guatemala under Arbenz in the earlier years of 1950 assumed a hostility quite out of proportion to the reality of events in both countries.

But race alone does not explain the "hostility" of such reporting, and it would be a gross violation of other elements intrinsic to the sphere of relations between Latin America and the U.S. to suggest so. There is a long history of conflict, both physical and ideological, between the two Americas, which the mass media reflect and like two peas in a pod, share the same landscape, but are quite different.

The U.S. has always persisted in a climate of enlightened idealism in its relations with other countries. But often accompanying it is an overbearing sense of moral rectitude, which fosters self-righteousness in itself and expects it in others. That this idealism is tainted cannot be seen but for the self-righteousness--a combination of the noble

84

idealism of the Enlightenment and the more austere
moral rectitude of Puritanism. Those countries which
fall short of this ideal are treated as fit subjects
for paternalism, and objects of perpetual scrutiny and
watchfulness. Latin America belongs to the first category and the Communist countries the second.

One writer suggests that there are three U.S. mass
media attitudes to Latin America: the colonial, the
technocratic and the hegemonic. 53/ The workings of
these three perspectives can be traced through the individual, the organization, and the national scene.
Individual attitudes towards news coverage in Latin
America influence that coverage; corporate identity and
its relations both to the individual and the state relates to news coverage and finally national policy and
its enactment and interaction with corporate power
affects news coverage. To what extent is the journalist, the corporate entity, or the mass media concerned
with the maintenance of the system? There is a view
that the connection is intimate and, perhaps, inseparable. 54/ Another view, which reflects the current
tendency to look at the field with the anthropologist's
eye, sees cultural influences in the news as unavoid-
able, given the differences between the Third World and
the industrialized countries. 55/

The information process cannot be separated from
the total productive, administrative and political
machinery of a country, in our view. It is indeed the
productive, administrative and political realities that
direct information and information flow. To pretend
that the flow of information is free and unfettered
misses the point. It can be free and it can be unfettered, but the images which result, spring from the
productive, administrative and political processes,
which originate at the corporate levels.

It is for this reason that current trends in communications research emphasize images which come from
the media rather than specific effects which result
from a given stimulus. 56/ Latin America, which has
in the past been cast in the role of victim of U.S.
cultural aggression, leads the renaissance in re-
appraising traditional models and devising non-
traditional approaches to information. Research questions include media ownership, public participation,
the ethics of the communications process, and social
questions such as race and religion. 57/ These questions form the nuclei of additional exercises aimed at

85

making communications research more relevant to their needs.

The research questions are influenced by ideological considerations and ideology is not value-free, but a commitment which can be either reformist or revolutionary. A total culture is examined and the differing roles of communication in national development identified. Gone, though not completely, is the dependence on facts and figures for universal validity. On the way out are vain glorious considerations of individual ability to change in the interests of conformity.

Latin American scholars share with others in the Third World a renewed concern for their societies and question the underlying mythology. Unlike fasionable researchers, they do not seek primarily to know the message and its use by the audience. They seek to know about the institution which produces the message, which is responsible for it. This sheds light on the power structure and the ideology of the power structure.

There is a distinct difference in how communication is seen by practitioners in the U.S. and how it is seen elsewhere. In the U.S. communication early was associated with measures designed to control behavior; in fact, scholars who developed and popularized the field were psychologists and sociologists, who approached the discipline as a response to the pressures of World War II; and propaganda warfare was not the least of their concerns. Previously though, at least one branch of the field was in the hands of the corporate structure, which sought to adjust the masses to the demands of consumption. 58/

Race, sex, class and ethnicity inevitably fit the pattern of a culture dedicated to individual gratification as rewards for conformism to material reality. The relationship of these factors, race, sex, etc., to material realities is a dialectic and "from this dialectic process sprang a culture peculiarly American--a culture in which ideas, images, values, and assumptions about human nature and society served specific ruling-class interests; they legitimized the capitalist economic system, for the ruled as well as the rulers." 59/ A wholistic view is discussed in a thoughtful work, 60/ and the consequence of it for black Americans, the subject of an equally searching analysis. 61/

The Third World, with its great diversity of cultures, must discover the social roots of mass culture. In order to do so, it must defend the fragility of its institutions against the challenge that comes from abroad and mainly from Anglo-American media. 62/ The response to this challenge underlines the significance of cultural imperialism. Many ingredients comprise cultural imperialism and each has its own distinct flavor. But men and machines are the main props of the system.

Notes

1/ Crowder, Michael. *West Africa Under Colonial Rule.* London: Hutchinson, 1966.

2/ Aronson, J. *The Press and the Cold War.* New York: Bobbs-Merrill, 1970.

3/ Halberstam, D. *The Best and the Brightest.* New York: Alfred Knopf, 1972.

4/ Shawcross, W. *Sideshow.* New York: Pocket Books, 1979.

5/ Galtung, J. & Ruge, M. "The Structure of Foreign News." *Journal of Peace Research.* Vol. 2. 1965.

6/ Hester, A. "An Analysis of News Flow from Developed and Developing Countries." *Gazette.* Vol. 17 (1, 2), 1971.

7/ Epstein, J. *News from Nowhere.* New York: Vintage Books, 1974. The author provides a revealing account of the institutional relationship between broadcast networks and professional schools.

8/ Flaherty, R. "Nanook." *In* L. Jacobs (ed.), *The Emergence of Film Art.* New York: Hopkinson & Blake, 1969. An absorbing documentary on human survival was *Nanook of the North.* Its Director, Robert Flaherty, was able to do this because he exposed himself over a ten-year period to the life of the Eskimos. Flaherty gives a moving account of his relationship to the Eskimos (p. 215).

9/ Himmelstrand, V. "The Problem of Cultural Translation in the Reporting of Africal Social Relities." *In* O. Stokke, *Reporting Africa.* New York: Africana Publishing Corporation, 1971.

10/ Knightley, P. *The First Casuality.* New York: Harcourt, Brace & Jovanovitch, 1981.

11/ *The New York Times*, October 1, 1979.

12/ The results of a study by Richard P. Nathan, Director of the Urban and Regional Research Center,

Princeton University, was reported in the <u>New York Times</u>, July 7, 1980.

<u>13</u>/ Leone de, R. <u>Small Futures</u>. New York: Harcourt, Brace, Jovanovich, 1979.

<u>14</u>/ V. S. Naipaul, the Caribbean novelist, chronicled with great acuity the plight of India in two books: <u>An Area of Darkness</u> and <u>A Civilisation Wounded</u>.

<u>15</u>/ <u>The New York Times</u>, October 1, 1979.

<u>16</u>/ <u>Ibid</u>., <u>The New York Times</u>, October 1, 1979.

<u>17</u>/ The difficulty of covering Africa can be even more difficult during times of crisis as the following account illustrates: "President Daniel arap Moi of Kenya warned news agencies based here to stop writing speculative stories on the war. He said the correspondents should leave Nairobi and go to Dar es Salaam or Kampala or 'indeed to the battlefield and get accurate and authentic news.' ...Frustrated at being so far from the scene, they (the journalists) have constructed a makeshift war room in a suite at the Inter-Continental Hotel, complete with maps and miniature tanks that shift position daily, more by inspiration than information." <u>The New York Times</u>, March 13, 1979.

<u>18</u>/ Segal, R. <u>The Race War</u>. New York: Viking Press, 1966, p. 27.

<u>19</u>/ Winks, R. <u>Chronicle for Higher Education</u>, October 9, 1979.

<u>20</u>/ Gans, H. <u>Deciding What's News</u>. New York: Pantheon, 1979, p. 338.

<u>21</u>/ Schlesinger, P. <u>Putting Reality Together</u>. London: Constable Press, 1978, p. 177, cited <u>in</u> Gans, H., "Deciding What's News."

<u>22</u>/ Gitlin, T. <u>The Whole World Is Watching: Mass Media in the Making and Unmaking of the New Left</u>. Berkeley, Calif.: University of California Press, 1980.

<u>23</u>/ Herbers, J. <u>The Lost Priority: What Happened to the Civil Rights in America</u>. New York: Funk & Wagnalls, 1970.

24/ Hopkins, J. "Racial Justice and the Press," MARC Paper, No. 1 (New York, Metropolitan Applied Research Center, 1968), p. 24.

25/ Goldsen, R. The Show and Tell Machine. New York: The Dial Press, 1977.

26/ Gross, B. Friendly Fascism. New York: M. Evans & Co., 1980.

27/ Epstein, J. Between Fact and Fiction. New York: Vintage Books, 1975, p. 215.

28/ Baestrup, P. How American Radio and Television covered the Tet Offensive in Vietnam and Washington in 1968. New York: Anchor Books, 1978.

29/ Op. cit., Gans, 1979.

30/ Both Columbia University and Harvard University have such programs.

31/ Op. cit., Bagdikian, 1971.

32/ Schiller, H. Mass Communication and American Empire. New York: Augustus M. Kelley, 1969.

33/ Op. cit., Epstein, 1975.

34/ Lippman, W. Public Opinion. New York: Crowell Collier & MacMillan, 1922.

35/ Dorman, W. A. and Omeed, E. "Reporting Iran the Shah's Way." Columbia Journalism Review. Jan.-Feb., 1979, pp. 27-33.

36/ Op. cit., Gans, H., 1979.

37/ Schiller, H. The Mind Managers. Boston: Beacon, 1973.

38/ Op. cit., Gross, 1980. To admit that this still persists is to move a step towards national salvation. Gross suggests that the educational system is responsible and the pressure to conform is so great that it narrows minds which might want to break out of its confines. In Beyond Culture, Edward T. Hall is even more pointed, laying the blame for national myopia squarely at the door of the educational system, which confuses education with learning, making the latter a painful exercise for most students at any age. The collective wisdom of Illich, Kozol and others contribute to the national concern for educational enlightenment and enrichment.

39/   Goldsen, R. The Television Environment. New York: The Dial Press, 1977.

40/   Tunstall, J. The Media are American. New York: Columbia University Press, 1977. The author writes: "One of the simplest but most important values of the Anglo-American media is status given to north European physical appearance (p. 90).

41/   Cole, B. and Oettinger, M. Reluctant Regulators. Mass.: Addison Wellesley, 1978. According to the authors, the renewal process is automatic if the applicant's papers are in order. "Less than 1 percent (0.0077) of processed applications went into hearing, and only one-quarter of 1 percent (0.0027), of applications was denied." (p. 134)

42/   Op. cit., Cole and Oettinger, 1978.

43/   Sandman, P., Rubin, D. & Sachsman, D. Media: An Introductory Analysis of American Mass Communications. N.J.: Prentice Hall, 1976.

44/   Report of the National Advisory Committee on Civil Disorders. New York: New York Times Co., 1968, p. 366.

45/   The Village Voice, May 21, 1979.

46/   The Amsterdam News, July 10, 1980.

47/   Op. cit., Report of the National Advisory Committee on Civil Disorders, 1978, p. 278.

48/   Fanon, F. The Wretched of the Earth. New York: Penguin Books, 1967.

49/   Memmi, A. The Colonizer and the Colonized. Mass., Boston: Beacon Press, 1972, p. 71.

50/   Horne, A. A Savage War of Peace. England, London: Penguin Books, 1979, p. 400.

51/   Andrew Young said: "If the three and a half million Palestinians are not accommodated in some way, their influence throughout the Arab world essentially will keep that region of the world distorted and upset ...it affects the flow of petroleum in this region of the world and when that begins to happen the prices go up, so does inflation, so does unemployment...There is no such thing as sticking to civil rights or to our domestic issues...that's not the kind of gospel we preach. We've reached the situation where in order to be liberated ourselves we must respond to the total liberation needs of people all over this planet. The New York Times, November 16, 1979.

52/ Francis, M. J. "The U.S. Press and Castro: A Study in Declining Relations." Journalism Quarterly, pp. 257-66.

53/ Pollock, J. C. An Anthropological Approach to Mass Communications Research: The U.S. Press and Political Change in Latin America. Latin American Research Review. Vol. 13, No. 1, 1978, p. 162.

54/ Rubin, B. Big Business and the Mass Media. Mass.: Lexington Books, 1977.

55/ Galtung, J. and Ruge, M. "The Structure of Foreign News." In J. Tunstall (eds.), Media Sociology: A Reader. Urbana: University of Illinois Press, 1977, p. 259.

56/ Gerbner, G. "Communication and Social Environment." In Communication: A Scientific American Book. San Francisco, Cal.: W. H. Freeman, 1972.

57/ Beltran, L. "Alien Promises." In Rogers, E. M. (eds.), Communication Research. Vol. 3, No. 2. April 1976, p. 115.

58/ Ewen, S. Captains of Consciousness. New York: McGraw Hill, 1977.

59/ Holt, T. C. "Probing the American Dilemma." Books and Arts. Washington, D.C.: November 1979.

60/ Takaki, R. Iron Cages. Race and Culture in 19th Century America. New York: Knopf, 1979.

61/ Cruise, H. The Crisis of the Negro Intellectual. New York: William Morrow & Co., 1967.

62/ Op. cit., Tunstall, 1977, p. 63.

Chapter 4

MAN AND MACHINES

Slowly but inexorably the Third World is being
deluged and strangled by a movement of men and machines from rich countries, peddling hard and soft ware
in the name of progress. In all of South America,
Africa and portions of Asia, this build-up of the
latest technological sophistication is pursued with un-
remitting relentlessness.

The Threat

Government, government-financed enterprises, international corporations, foundations, universities
and private industry partake in a profitable concern
which disposes of huge profits, involves traffic in
highly-skilled personnel, international agreements,
and a turnover in the knowledge business that touches
the humanities and science departments of leading universities.

The peddlers of technology assume that they are
indeed welcome and will always be so, for who can deny
the obvious benefits that hold true for a society,
which is devoted to technology. They do not always
question the need for technology, nor do they estimate
the results of their efforts. And since they ask no
questions, they can provide inadequate answers to the
many and pressing questions that accompany the introduction of technology.

In any case, feedback mechanism is frequently un-
available or sophisticated. It is therefore impossible
for them to forecast the future of a society into which
technology has been suddenly introduced--and Iran comes
readily to mind. But that, they will say, is surely
not their objective. While their remote objectives are
to bring about the progress (they identify progress
with prosperity), their immediate objectives are to
achieve this through swift change on economic, political and cultural levels.

Central to this is the belief that technology is
desirable for its own sake and, what is more, given the
circumstances in which the country finds itself, the
only answer to a multitude of woes. Thus, increasingly

technology is used to bring about change in education, to speed industrial growth and to refurbish generally.

In the haste towards progress, rich countries have come to believe that the rest of the world, and in particular Third World countries should willy-nilly emulate their approach towards the entire paraphernalia of technology and communication. The TW, which is indeed the offspring of the twentieth century, should be the inheritor of its tools. Besides, they believe that the pressures that operate on Third World countries--nation-building, instability, economic dependency, education, unemployment, relative industrial incapacity--should impel them to utilize the swiftest means available to eliminate poverty.

The rich countries see change as inevitable and advantageous if it is comprehensive rather than piecemeal. Central to change is balance and equilibrium; the distribution of wealth between the urban and country dwellers, the blue collar and the white collar workers, the privileged and the underprivileged, those able to afford the trappings of technology and those unable to; balance among political factions that will inherit the new gods and share in its blessings. These elements of change and what they protend for the future have to be examined.

But Third World countries cannot afford unrestricted change. Because of the resources and skilled manpower industrialized countries can afford the luxury of indiscriminate technological change; others less rich, are not in a position to do this. Even if the latter are, it is questionable whether it is in their interests so to do. This, unfortunately, is not realized and damage done cannot be corrected. For how is it possible to estimate qualitatively the violence done a culture, or damage to the human sector? It is dangerous to commit a country to high-level technology before the problems which inevitably accompany it are studied.

In the mass media of communication, for example, certain well-documented reports and papers appear in the pages of UNESCO bulletins; the Ivory Coast television project, those in San Salvador and Colombia; and also programs sponsored by private agencies such as Telstar in Zaire. Much of the work done is well-intentioned but not comprehensive and traditional

94

educational methods persist in situations demanding new and fresh approaches.

What is needed is a theory adequate to and in harmony with the needs of the country, one which takes stock of its social and cultural background and which will contain rather than be contained by technology; moreover, a theory which considers individual welfare as the essential ingredient of constructive social change. Theory must come before practice in the race to change people's habits and attitudes. For a not-inconsiderable morality is involved in any attempt to manipulate human beings. For who will bear the responsibility for human relations? The behavioral scientists as well as the politician must share the responsibility. But it is humanity that will in the final analysis bear the responsibility for human relations, not technology.

Technology of culture or culture of technology

Technology with its enormous appetite has become an integral part of cultural exports to the Third World. Private enterprise and government, deeply committed to it, are alive to the possibility of increased social and political hegemony. Nowhere is this more evident than in the telecommunications industry, which has close links to foreign policy. 1/

Culture as diplomacy by other means is very much the basis of present educational and cultural relations. 2/ One writer considers three stages in the cultural relations between nations. The first stage is haphazard and without apparent plan and occurs as a result of chance meeting. The second stage is commonly associated with imperialistic expansion which is both "a motive as well as a consequence of war." Culture is an instrument of national glorification and hegemony, a supporter of ethnocentrism and self-righteousness. The third stage, the present era, is characterized by increased contact and greater depth and persuasiveness and culture becomes not merely the province of government, but also of other institutions which share in the general cultural exchange--richness in diversity.

But this view does not square with the realities of modern communications technology. It is relatively simple for the science and technology industry, its

95

prowess refined by a multiplicity of foreign engage-
ments--Korea, Vietnam as well as space conquests--to
harness its strengths for peaceful cultural penetration. Moreover, the increasing tendency for government administrations to become more powerful, has
pushed other institutions to comply. The business of
culture is shared by many; but policy at both official
and unofficial levels is determined by those who control the output of technology. A unanimity of outlook
operates at the policy and decision-making levels, even
though differences in the implementation of policy may
be tolerated. A coherence of view about objectives
exists in the corridors of power which makes it still
easier for policy to be carried out.

Cultural penetration is easiest when there is un-
questioning faith in mission. The mission of policy-
makers is to spread a way of life to those who accept
it and increasingly to those who would not. Devotion
to this ideal is truly messianic. Wealth and power
breed an aggressive nationalism that reinforces cultural imperialism. The dynamism of the alien culture,
makes it incapable of sympathizing with with the host
culture, however noble the intentions of the former.
A narrow ethnocentrism blinds and dulls minds, so that
it distracts from wholesome objectives. The potentiality which rich countries have for doing this is indeed
gargantuan; and the capacity for offense is only equal
to that of annoyance, which leaves behind a trail of
bitterness.

This unchecked onslaught of technological know-how
does violence to cultural values which include all that
is known, held sacred, believed, honored and revered by
indigenous masses. The heritage that is handed down
from one generation to another, represents the sum total of the experiences of that society, and any theory
of development that does not incorporate them is incomplete and does not support national integrity.

How can the poor countries with the benefits of
technology without sacrificing those irreplaceable
elements of their own cultural experience? How can
they prevent what Fanon refers to as "the epidermali-
zation of this inferiority complex," and how can they
withstand this "cultural imposition." 3/

Fanon's point is complex. First, it is a warning
against the evils of unchecked technological expansion. Second, it is a call to salvage from the past

96

those elements that best help their countries overcome
the technological explosion. And it may well be that
to do this effectively, the TW will have to employ
those parts of technology that seem least to threaten
institutions and the lives of their citizens. Hopefully, out of this will come a faith that sustains
against pressures from outside and renews from within.
For technology affects whole societies and raises fundamental questions. Its prowess is accompanied by radical changes in the lives of people, affects their
work, how they arrange time, and how they spend their
leisure. This profound social upheaval has immense
consequences for poor countries which can never return
to the status quo. Not only is there dislocation economically and politically, but also in the human psyche.
But mankind has tackled challenges like this before and
there is an enormous potential for ingenuity and adap-
tability. Today is but yesterday writ large. Only by
guarding against false images that distract and idols
of the marketplace can these countries pass on to their
people a legacy that is their own.

Technology, social change and
the Third World

     Technological innovation influences social change.
The proliferation of modern technology has resulted in
an inability to effectively conceptualize, define,
understand, and predict the process of social change.
Almost as soon as people begin to adapt to changes in
technology, whole new paraphernalia replace the old,
and the entire cycle of adaptation begins anew. 4/
Though there are things common to both old and new,
their impact cannot readily be assessed. While history
may be a useful tool for looking at old and new, past
and present, it provides a restricted yardstick.

     There is a tendency to see the world of change in
terms of technology. We are led quite falsely to study
social change by examining technology; also, we com-
pare present society to that which existed prior to the
introduction of a particular form of technology. This
method is as limited as the historical method. Both
yield a statistic that avails nothing, for we employ
a technical standard for measuring a human process.
Man, not technique, is the fulcrum for the study of
social change.

     As man and his culture are integral to the en-
vironment, cultural change is a necessary ingredient

97

of any social change. Technology has destroyed traditional yardsticks for observing cultural change by substituting "technique" for culture. Today, it is more accurate to speak in terms of a culture of technique than a culture per se, as culture is becoming increasingly defined in technical terms. Because of this, we may consider the culture of technology through factors that explain any cultural change. Four such exist: recognition, synthesis, dissemination and absorption. 5/ Each factor is a process in itself, but is by no means self-contained, or isolated; rather, each leads progressively to the next.

Recognition

Recognition might include not only physical objects, e.g., television sets, books, tools etc., but also, for example, scientific formulae for the manufacture of the hydrogen bomb. Both physical and nonphysical artifacts are significant parts of present day culture. The splitting of the atom has opened up new and exciting possibilities for science and in turn a culture based on science. The recognition of elements that contribute to our culture is influenced by the demand for them. The physical destruction caused by the atomic bomb awoke us to the sober reality of an Armageddon and thus the need for constructive measures to save humanity. This paved the way for governments to consider peaceful uses of the atom. Need for regulation spurred demand for it.

Synthesis

Synthesis occurs when the existing culture incorporates a new element within its boundaries; that is, the culture does not reject the new element. That element is therefore able to establish a base within the existing framework of a society because of its usefulness and practical value to it. The proliferation of the automobile in countries that can afford it is an example. But synthesis does not imply complete agreement; groups within the social structure might reject an artifact or they might accept with reservation. Acceptance of a new element by a majority of the population is sufficient to ensure its place in that society.

Dissemination

When elements of a given culture are publicized, they tend to appear elsewhere. This occurs mainly through influential groups which spread the message and promote its acceptance to a wider public. It also happens when a majority of people finds those elements to its liking, or when cultural artifacts themselves do their own promotion and gain admission to a new culture, without having to be filtered through groups. Fragments of the culture of technology of the U.S. have gained widespread currency in Third World countries precisely this way.

The dissemination of the culture of technology is facilitated by the mass media of communication and indirectly by the ease and regularity with which people travel from place to place. Television, radio and film by extending horizons promote an interest in travel. Circulation of printed material, and other kinds of communication technology narrows the borders of the world community, causing increased possibilities for human interaction. Technology, therefore, rapidly spreads from one culture to another, especially from an industrial country to a non-industrial one, as the trend increasingly seems.

Significant for the Third World is that its cultural base is threatened by a culture of technology, which is able to rely on rapid transit through the communications media.

Absorption

Elements of an alien culture can very rapidly infiltrate a host country and become absorbed and by means of the mass media. These go directly to the people, without having to go through influential leaders or groups unless the latter controls the media. And as the mass media attract, the content of messages is more readily acceptable and therefore received without too much question.

The media break down social barriers and destroy the often delicate balance within a country, creating the need for new social adjustments. Constant adjustments take place and renovation, disorganization, or disequilibrium results. Faced with a constant barrage

of cultural diversity, adequate defences must be employed. When cultural domination becomes calculated
policy, this is cultural imperialism.

Third World: View of Technology

Despite caveats about technology, points of view
about its usefulness are generally positive. Technology is seen as helping to bridge that all important
gap between rich and poor, enabling those countries
that exist on the borderline of prosperity to become
more competitive and those which are poor to overcome
poverty.

The Third World sees technology as a means to redress a balance that colonial and other forms of domination had visibly upset. For not only are they heirs
to an underdeveloped economic and political status, but
also, more often than not, an underdeveloped educational system as well. Moreover, leaders of the Third
World look avidly to technology to help them fulfil the
often outrageous promises made to an electorate at national elections. The paraphernalia of modern technology have been pressed into service in South America,
Africa, Asia, especially in the most crucial area of
education; and technology is of immeasurable assistance
to national planners faced with urgent national problems.

The application of technological methods represents
a reassuring confidence in technology. Science is involved in the task of immediate attainment of certain
objectives, and as far as this is true, supports the
view that technology benefits mankind. This is especially true for "developing" man who must utilize technology simply to remain in the race against time.
Above all, science and technology are seen as the great
liberalizing influence of our time, bringing a knowledge of skills, and at least, a certain prosperity。

Technology: A positive view

Apologists for technology are heirs to the tradition of Western philosophy culminating in nineteenth
century liberal philosophers, who saw science as a
study to influence, if not to control, human destiny.
Mathematics, scientific method were held as supreme
examples of rational and therefore objective thinking.
It is a spectrum of intellectual history that included
Newton, Darwin, Malthus, Saint-Simon, Comte and

Descartes that crystallized during the Industrial Revolution and gained currency in America, which was its
testing ground.

Supporters of the new technological age defend it
on the grounds that the appearance of sub-cultures
prevent any tendency towards conformity and standardi-
zation. They see in it a greater freedom for mankind
and a release of creative new energies. But people in
the Third World cannot look forward to this barely disguised Utopian concept for a number of reasons.

First, because they are generally unable as yet to
provide themselves with their own home-spun version of
technology across a wide range of activities, though
there is some promise in that direction. 6/ Technological man, as conceived by Western nations, is still
very much of an unknown for a significant part of the
world. Second, the new technology comes from the "outside" for the most part, and it has to contend with that
easily attached label "Western" or "Eastern" with all
the value judgments that follow. This makes it less
acceptable in the long-run than the home-grown product.
Acceptance of technology is in large measure influenced
by the society that produces it. This is so for a most
definite reason unadmitted by the apologists for technological man.

The economic and political revolution in the Third
World is in process. These countries are still actively engaged in self-discovery and the formation of national images. As they progress towards their objectives highly technologized countries also move forward,
but at a swifter rate. The initial gap is still very
much present. Third World countries might never close
it and never be able to provide themselves with those
positive aspects of technology for their own purposes.

Technology: A negative view

There are those who take an opposite view of technology: a negative view. They say that while technology supports the human condition, its main objective
is the production of more goods. They argue that the
upgrading of education is not for a socially useful
end in itself, but rather to promote an educated elite
better able to perform in a society geared to increased
productivity. Those opposed to technology see this as
a weakening of the human condition and as having a deleterious effect. Technological man, as they envisage

101

him, is a mere cog in the wheel of industry, losing the main purpose of his being and thus alienated from himself. Technology is portrayed as striving to over-reach itself and adopting measures aimed at perpetuating its interests. This results in increased centralization and soul less bureaucracy, accompanying other measures designed to induce, if not compel, total human compliance with official policy. Governments then come under the sway of an economic hierarchy and forcefully stamp out pockets of resistance as they develop among the retractors. A situation approximating Fritz Lang's "Metropolis" is foreseen, where a state becomes the epitome of industrialization, where every effort bends to the wheels of industry, and humanity lost, becomes inhuman and treacherous.

The roots of alienation are, of course, romantic; from Rousseau to latter-day existentialists like Marcuse, the philosophical goal is to prevent the separation of man from himself and from nature. This view holds that the more deeply involved man becomes with industrialization, the further removed he is from his own precious identity. Industrialization is an evil, not always necessary, for the fulfillment of certain specialized goals, which falsely relate to health and happiness. Man is thought to be more prepared to countenance these factors if they seem directly relevant to what he is about, if they do not impinge on his daily activity, or if they do not prevent his own creative development.

But the mass production of goods that accompanies advanced technology, conspires to stifle ends; more and more man as worker, as citizen, becomes wrapped up in the ordinary demands made upon him by society. Caught up in the webb of production, bureaucracy, enforced routine and inadequate leisure, man is said to become estranged from his "true" nature and increasingly sinks into a kind of spiritless cocoon with little hope of self-actualization. Politically, he is never more at the mercy of an elite capable of manipulating him to whatever governing philosophy it espouses. Further, those who oppose technology maintain that man surrenders his will for limited security, which is not really security, but paralysis of body and mind. Unable to think creatively, he supports those who can, or whom he imagines can, believing that he expresses his own will through them, in much the same way that a voter believes that his representative expresses his

102

wishes at tribunal level; but the opposite is also true, that the representative, in expressing himself, believes that he is acting out the wishes of the people he claims to represent. But technological man is incapable of thinking in such sophisticated terms, for he has long since grown passive. His wants satisfied, his physical comforts looked after, his limited pleasures prescribed, he is the subject of his own security; but unlike Aristotle's primemover he has no grace.

Such is the state of man in "Brave New World." A man who has ceased to live because he has abandoned the will to live by his own creed. When realization did come, it was too late to do anything about it, for by that time he had become a virtual prisoner in the society he himself helped to create. His next best choice was to become an integral functioning unit of that society; he joined forces with tyranny to dehumanize his fellow men and in the act further dehumanized himself.

Note here, the suggested alliance between machine society and the political process. In order to ensure the profitability of the machine, the society is whipped into line by conventional politics--the politics of conservatism. The political system is indescribable, for to describe is to define and to define is to attribute form and content to substance. A faceless elite, fearful of itself, rules an equally faceless society; and since that elite is always fearful of those within the society that do not conform, a climate of suspicion prevails. In such an atmosphere nothing is clear-cut. Issues are kept blurred, for even to admit that there are issues is to detract attention from the business at hard, which is to keep the machine going.

Politics reflects the confining sameness of dull routine; and power and wealth become the sole criteria for that society. In the beginning power is held by the technocrats who manage the intricate relationships, which accompany a society dominated by the machine. Because of the wealth which accumulates, a network of relationships develops, forcing those in power to broaden its base to include the bureaucracy responsible for them. This sacrifice aimed at facilitating government does not in fact aid government. It creates a subsidiary class no less suspicious than the original power structure; perhaps more so, since it enjoys only the shadow and not the substance. Unable

103

to enjoy the trappings of real power, it frustrates itself by its own inadequacy.

The elite becomes aware of rising discontentment within and seeks a remedy by the addition of more creature comforts. While these persist, there is superficial happiness: superficial because comforts are another factor in alienation, as they separate man from nature and emphasize the material at the expense of the mental. By whatever means the elite strives to perpetuate the status quo, it cannot guarantee it, for technology itself is changing both in quality and scope. Measures to control deviant behavior are ad hoc and lack universality. While oppressive measures stifle revolt, they do not avail against withdrawal and are only barely successful against despondency.

Critics of technology see a gloomy future for man living within a technologically produced mass society. 7/ Moreover, they believe that such a society can have no main objective upon which a majority of the people agree.

For the Third World, the problem of alienation is critical for internal cohesiveness and economic and political development. Take black Africa for instance: three interacting elements might produce alienation: African culture, Western culture and what they both give rise to. Loss of identity is the price of progress as Western cultural norms infiltrate the society. Traditional culture is driven out and superseded by Western culture. The admixture of the two prophesized by Malinowski has yet to take place. What he did not indicate was a mass culture that would follow the introduction of the mass media and the questions of adjustment to individual freedom of action that would arise.

What we do not know is whether the liberation inherent in the new technology, vividly prophesized and which has not been conspicuously successful in the U.S., will alleviate the problems that accompany it. 8/ Or, will the new technology simply compound the effects of the old industrialism. Assuredly, it seems to us that there is reason enough to be cautious about the wholesale adoption of methods, however efficacious, in tackling some of the social, economic, and political problems of the Third World.

Technology: A neutral view

Another school of thought is of the opinion that
since technology is an integral part of the social process, judgment must be postponed until the whole social
structure is evaluated. Technology, this view says, is
simply another factor in social change, among others.
In any event, runs the argument, technology alone is at
best a rough index of social change. Society is constantly changing and diverse ingredients and properties
contribute their fair share in a proportion commen-
surate with their capacities, ambitions, influence.

Most societies are like this and adjustments accompany the introduction of new products and inventions.
Indeed, the value of a new product is dependent on the
ability of people to recognize a need for it. That
alone tells us something about mental attitudes towards
receptability of new things. For instance, the wheel
came at a time when the mental disposition to new ideas
generated its own demand for them. This is why technology poses no insuperable problem to a society in which
it is introduced, whether it comes from outside or from
within.

Human resources and their attributes--language,
habit, social organization--came before technology.
Man, as Protagorus said, "is the measure of all things;"
and just as he accommodated the wheel and the printing
press into his daily routine, he will do the same with
modern tools. Man adjusts not only because he has to,
but because he wants to.

This view is attractive, because it simplifies the
debate by placing man at the center of the argument.
In so doing it strives to accommodate those critics who
see man held captive in the grip of the machine. It
has the same appeal as does Marx for naive planners who
look to him for salvation. But just as Marx did not
foresee that the disappearance of capitalism might cause
the emergence of a class that was neither capitalist
nor politerian, but in fact a kind of efficient elite,
so the defenders of this view cannot envision the numerous features of a modern technology that do not leave
much room for individual detachment. 9/

Traditional methodology is found wanting in the
face of such alarming possibilities. New perspectives
for dealing with this avalance of alternatives are yet
to develop. Thus, in the U.S., the growth of

technology outdistances the ability to develop new ways of tackling it. Institutions have not been geared for the new era and there is a considerable gap between what we currently are and what we might become. Just as the rise of industrialism in the nineteenth century was accompanied by a great deal of human suffering, so the new era of technology is accompanied by a plethora of problems of anxieties. Because of hasty utilization we have not developed the means for fully understanding their potential. A limited perspective sees only immediate gains or individual gratification, a wider vista escapes us. This is because of the customary individual response to stimulus as opposed to collective social action. Essentially, it is an economic value system that has its roots in the free enterprise society.

This is not to imply that individual enterprise has not been altruistic, or cannot be so, or that the profit motive is incompatible with social action; but such altruism as there is, enhances possibilities for further wealth accumulation. Time and effort is not spent on innovations to buttress a society, or indeed, a civilization, against forces that would drastically change it. It may well be that the concept of technology for humanity must be "packaged" and "sold" like any commodity in order to stimulate sluggish minds to action.

Technology must be seen as an integral part of the social process and an offshoot of human creativity. Technology is new knowledge whose social and political implications cannot be ignored; and by restricting it to narrow economic considerations, stifles present development and arrests future possibilities.

Concentration on the economic ramifications of technology--dirty cities, unhealthy living conditions, smog, water pollution, labor dislocation--emphasize the untoward effects at the expense of the beneficial, thereby providing fuel for the critics of technological growth, and swelling the ranks of those who see the quality of human life imperiled.

One popular view of widespread currency concerns automation. According to this view, automation brings about varying degrees of unemployment, if not total displacement. This notion is an understandable over-reaction, but it does not consider other factors.

First, while automation does cause a number of jobs to be abolished, it does tend to create new positions which partially compensate for the loss of jobs. Second, upgrading of workers through education opens new horizons for men whose jobs are eliminated. The net loss, however, is compensated for by a net gain of new positions elsewhere in the labor market. But this assumes ideal conditions; that is, full employment. When conditions are not ideal, a labor market that is less than perfect, can very seriously affect efforts of displaced workers to find jobs.

Automation does not incur such anxieties in the Third World. The implications of technology on social change will have to be studied from terms of reference indigenous to the countries concerned. What we do not wish to see is a repetition of past errors, which can with reasonable foresight, be avoided. What technologically advanced countries and the Third World have in common is that all social change brought about through technology will not only occasion immense upheaval but also future expansion.

The challenge of technology

Present benefits are as important as future possibilities. The idealistic individualism that is so much a feature of the uses of technology in the U.S., has withheld studied assessment of the future. This results in a state where its growth threatens to surpass the ability to harness its advances in the common interest. Reaction is therefore ex post facto. The telephone is a useful instrument for social intercourse, but it is also a means for the invasion of privacy. The assembly line is an indispensable element in the mass production of creature comforts--automobiles, television sets, appliances--but it causes alienation among workers.

A crisis of confidence in the ability to harness technology in the service of humanity exists. Belatedly, and with indecent haste, legislation has been introduced to curb the rampant ill effects of unchecked technological growth. This reveals inadequate planning at the corporate level and a conspicuous incapacity to project beyond immediate gains. If "gains" are coincident with the well-being of society, a case can be made for self-regulatory measures within the corporate structure. But this is not so.

The business of technology cannot be the exclusive preoccupation of technocrats or industrialists. Because it involves everybody, and development in one quarter has a corresponding effect elsewhere, appraisal must be widespread.

Increasingly, the Third World is host to technological innovations as they diffuse from western or other countries in the form of development aid or capital investment. They are participants in a very recent tradition, whose roots have scarcely been established. There is no reason to believe that capitalists and investors will be guided by any more social awareness in their dealings with these countries. In fact, there is some evidence that the opposite might be true: ethnocentrism, racism and a disguised cynicism sometimes characterize attitudes towards these new countries. And, because of the social and political pressures existing within the Third World, there is the likelihood of repetition of past errors. This is particularly true if Third World countries are not alive to the dangers.

Each new era feels the need to reinforce belief in its own newness and uniqueness. The present technological era is no exception. Technology makes swift and impermanent social changes. We do not know where we are going. We cannot construct an adequate defense, for we do not know from what angle the attack will come. The most we can do is to prepare our societies for change wherever that change might come from.

The Third World has not yet established a sophisticated warning system; each country has a way of life and a culture to protect against the inhuman exploitation of technology unchecked. But each also has the opportunity to create new systems, uninfluenced by private corporate structures that exercise so much weight. While western countries are in the final stages of industrialization, Third World countries have just begun. Mass communication has made it easy for barriers to come down, but it has also made it all the more difficult to defend traditional institutions and life-styles.

Few political leaders are unaware of the gigantic possibilities for revolutionizing the economy of their countries through exploitation of national resources; many of these leaders welcome whatever the "new" knowledge brings. Adaptation of indigenous institutions is quietly taking place with only the more pronounced aspects being visible. New kinds of relationships are developing in the midst of social change: between members of a family that have come to live in a city; in a village in which television has suddenly pierced the quiet of the night. Technology hastens change but of crucial importance is the speed and smoothness with which local institutions adapt to pressures within them.

The challenge of technology in the Third World does not lie in the development of sophisticated machinery alone. Rather it is the priority that is placed on human resources. Will humanity gain or will it lose? Technology can serve both ends. The question is which end will it serve.

Politics and technology

The continuing plight of the poor and hungry of the Third World has attracted the attention of the world. But unless there is understanding of the limits of technology, what it has to offer can be lost, leaving only a catalogue of mistakes and hardships, such as attended the introduction of the industrial revolution of the nineteenth century. Refined social and political structures are needed to channel input and monitor progress.

There are two reasons for this. First, in order to ensure that what it has to offer is diffused to all the people and not to a privileged elite. Second, to prevent the domination of economic and social considerations over political and cultural ones. Because of a lack of private entrepreneurs, governments will have to take an increasing role in regard to the setting up of these structures; on the other hand, as government departments can be bureaucratic and confining, it might be simpler to set up an independent agency with government support, rather than place it directly under a ministry or government department. There is need for this especially as bureaucratic structures have generally not kept pace with national development.

Technology in colonial times

In most of black Africa, for example, political structures, even when adapted to the present day, are a hangover from an era of altogether limited needs. These were designed to serve the requirements of a colonial era, in which local participation was at best minimal. Essentially, these colonial territories were providers and not participants and it is wrong to suggest that colonialism prepared local administrations for leadership and for service to the state. In fact, the opposite is true. Such education in political arts as were transmitted either by osmosis or design (to aid the perpetuation of colonial power) aimed almost exclusively at making administration more efficient and therefore in the long run, more productive, for the imperialist. 10/

Vestiges of the past still remain. True, changes were made conversant with local interests and parochial loyalties, but these essentially were in the form of additives or appendages to a colonial structure by leaders who, despite radical views, were sufficiently part of the colonial system to be confined and limited by it. It is only when this heritage is discovered to be incongruent with urgent and pressing developmental demands that revision takes place.

Then, too, we must not overlook the commendable foresight of colonial powers, which, on the eve of withdrawal, saw fit to encourage those institutions that supported their own future machinations.

But these plans did not long carry. Inevitably, they could not stand the rigid test of buoyant, self-conscious nationalism, in some quarters; and again they failed to take into account the future leadership that would bend tradition to suit its own purposes. They failed to foresee also that artificiality in political management is not an effective substitute for indigenous radicalism. The Nigerian civil war was a commentary on the ineffectiveness of a constitution, which did not safeguard the interests of a total people; and in so far as it did, sowed the seeds for a balkanization, which was to have such tragic consequences.

Nigeria is significant because it proves that traditional structures cannot immediately adapt to searching political realities; moreover, as technology brings about change, these institutions were not therefore sufficiently flexible to incorporate the expansion that accompanies social, economic and political changes.

Much of the current instability in some African countries stems from the inability to recognize the limitations of effete institutions which, though

workable in colonial times, need revision because of
new circumstances. This dependence on colonial machinery stems from a prevailing view of the Third
World, and Africa in particular, that Western organizations are superior to those of other nations and
therefore worth copying. 11/ This attitude is especially discernible in the persisting view of these countries as "underdeveloped," "developing," and "emerging."
These labels cannot be disassociated from the value
judgments implicit in their use. The tragedy is that
they have given rise to almost permanent mental attitudes, which resist understanding precisely what is
"underdeveloped," "developing," and "emerging." They
also reveal a startling ignorance of historical and
other factors, which lead to the present. How much this
is a product of shoddy investigation, a lack of it, or
a misguided intellect fearful of the consequences of
systematic research, is difficult to tell. Certainly,
there is convincing evidence of Africa's own ability
to develop her own resources, taming nature in the process. 12/

It was nearly two million years ago that the first
tool was made in Tanzania and from this humble beginning dictated by necessity, emerged a sophisticated
system of social organization. But this is beyond the
scope of this present work. Development is therefore
relative not only to the age in which it takes place,
but also to the social environment; and those who consider "development" as a state of mobility from being
to becoming, omit the essential fact that development
has always been taking place under different stages.

Industrial expansion in the Western world in the
nineteenth century paralleled the development of new
political structures; indeed, it might be safely said
that this expansion brought about significant change
politically. A whole school of factory, health and
educational legislation was inspired by the need to
rectify some of the more obnoxious consequences of industrial progress. The point here is that social and
economic expansion requires the introduction of new
structures.

The need for this in the Third World is more than
crucial, for technology will surely outstrip those establishments that were geared for different and less
pressing circumstances. The paradox is that the two
institutions which promoted structural change in the

111

Western world were those that were "centered" in Africa
--the slave trade and slavery in the new world.

But they also brought changes. The colonial system demanded and obtained national subservience to its
aims and total exploitation could only take place if
the entire society was brought into line. Whatever expansion that took place during the European nineteenth
century invasion was structured to meet the requirements of the overseas economy. Commercial and industrial systems were designed to facilitate the exploitation of the resources of the colonized. Improved
standards of living in the colonial countries were
directly related to industrial and commercial enterprises in the colonial empires.

As a supplier of raw materials, African institutions underwent change in the interests of greater efficiency. Whatever modernization took place, for example, in transport, communications and power, also
supported the general economic ideas of the time. The
impact of industrialization was beginning to be felt,
and in consequence, Africa's modern expansion kept
pace with economic demands made upon her by alien rule.
Reorganization of economies and political power accompanied increased demands: centralization of political
spheres of influence and attendant concentration of
power rather than its diffusion, illustrated the prevailing economic urgency; and as these changes were
conceived in haste, and indifferent attention paid to
social equilibrium or political nicety, they could not
pretend to be considered as structural changes. They
were designed with a particular purpose in view, without consideration of how that purpose related to the
whole system in operation. In so far as colonialism
was deliberate policy, it depended upon the skills of
administrators and the military for implementation.
As the system widened, becoming more complex, understanding how to work it also grew, until a fairly
sophisticated body of knowledge, based on the practical
experiences of administrators, coalesced into theory.

But the colonial system did bring Western technology in mechanized form: railways were built for
transportation of raw materials to ports; and miners
were exploited. There is little evidence, however,
that this technology filtered through the society. In
fact, colonial policy did now allow the natives to
share in the fruits of this industrial and highly profitable Western expansion, until much later.

There were many elements that stood in the way of the new knowledge filtering through: ruthless race discrimination, which prevented any but the most superficial contact between laborers and their white managers; an innate belief that the native was somehow unable to learn any but the most mundane skills; and a desire to keep even these from him--impelled no doubt by fear that he could not be trusted with secrets of the inner workings of the machine, or, more probably that he could, thus destroying the basis of racial superiority.

Yet contact did exist, and those who vigorously opposed interaction, were often the staunchest beneficiaries of it. The system, which often rigidly excluded participation by Africans, could not in fact survive without them; and in maintaining the system, they learned a great deal about it. But interaction took place on the periphery. Machines, whatever their productivity, never reached the stage, where they could completely be assimilated in the society. A distinction, an unconscious one perhaps, was made between that which brought physical benefits and that which did not, between the material and the spiritual.

Technology was separate from humanity, and the former was at no time allowed to impose itself on community life, though in fact it did later on, as migrants from the villages increasingly came to the industrial centers in search of work. Then, skill began to play a significant part in the ability to obtain employment, for obviously a person of skills would find it easier to gain employment. But in any case, as there was no definitive plan to help people to procure the necessary skills, there was not an overabundance of applicants in this category.

Despite this disequilibrium, rural people flocked to the industrial centers in search of unskilled, low-paid labor and such minimal prosperity as they enjoyed, and aggravated the problems which came in the wake of industrialization. There were never the amenities that we have to take for granted in towns and urban centers, and little or no provision was made to accommodate the migrants, who flocked in from the villages and rural areas. The new arrivals were displaced persons in a very real sense. The introduction of industrialization by the colonial powers was accompanied by human suffering on a scale unknown in nineteenth

113

century Europe, the more, so as there wasn't the possibility of redress of grievances. In Europe, the development of trade unions paralleled industrial expansion; in the colonies, they were not encouraged.

The physical discomforts of these towns apart, the new industrial underclass encountered other difficulties. They were uprooted from the security of their villages and transplanted in an alien environment, which previous experience had not conditioned them to adjust to. But if the newly arrived could not readily acclimatize, they soon became-aware of new, though restricted possibilities for individual advancement. It provided the young with the chance to evade traditional responsibilities and to acquire new life-styles. The older among them were unable to change fundamental attitudes and restricted change; but the conflict between traditional elements and the more adventurous provided stimulus for change.

As a result, new kinds of relationships came into being; as the rural communities became less productive --because of the flight to industrial areas--the transformation of the towns, or more properly, logies, into viable dwelling units began. The juxtaposition of heterogenous elements caused friction and security of group loyalties was hard put to withstand the pressures of the early urban communities.

It must not be inferred that towns were a recent creation in Africa, or that the creation of the first towns brought about social dislocation; but there is a substantial difference between those that were the product of local efforts, and those that haphazardly came into being as a result of colonial expansion. In a sense, the young industrial mass thrown together in assorted groups to work the mines, was the start of a demonstrable political awareness. Inevitably, they would learn to sink their differences in the face of the need to mobilize against the alien power; inevitably, they would band together to form trade unions and political groups; inevitably, too, as an educated fringe, lucky enough to either be sent abroad for schooling, or receive it from missionaries, they would want to aspire to distant heights. The rise of political leadership in Africa coincides with the industrial expansion that took place in the colonial era. The industrial towns with their suffering humanity, provided a stage for talents and organization became the password. It is significant that early

114

politicization took the form of organization into trade unions to demand higher wages and better living conditions. And trade unions played a decisive role in the independence movement.

Industrialization, while bringing limited benefits, also helped to destroy rural life, without significantly contributing to the material advancement of those who had left the rural areas. In fact, such urban centers as were established could not prosper, for the conditions of prosperity did not exist (in part they did, but not for the natives and wages were too low to promote any but marginal living and even food became an expensive commodity, as there was nobody left in the rural districts to work the land).

Workers in industry amassing substantial wealth for overseas empires, contributed to the death of the rural economies by absence from the land. They could not in any way adequately support their families who remained behind, nor could they provide the stimulus for effective local administration. The migrant workers in urban districts became contributors to rural poverty. There was not only economic poverty but also institutional poverty.

Nor was there any hope that the recent-created urban centers could flourish under the existing conditions. To begin with, employment was precarious, for it tended to fluctuate with consumer demand abroad. Required but not implemented was integration of the industrial process with agricultural diversification. What resulted from this shortsighted economic policy was a complete separation of industrialization from the rural agriculture, town from village and the corresponding absence of any political machinery to effect a fusion of interests. The problem was further compounded by the dislocation of village life, because workers were unable to take their families with them to the towns, and the breakdown of traditional values that was at the heart of the village. This crisis in the villages was only equalled by that in the towns, where workers, unable to feel part of a crippling industrial community, attracted and were attracted by all the miseries that accompany industrialization--petty crime, and prostitution.

Industrialization was forced into an already bankrupt system, which had perilously few ideas, and these only to perpetuate itself, or in the event of withdrawal, to leave some structure behind that would continue in the old ways. But it would be wrong to consider the colonial period of industrialization as an evil in itself. A system is capable of only so much expansion and new ideas must be brought in when circumstances change. But the colonial system could not itself bring about any considerable change, for good; to do so would be to deny that it was synonymous with exploitation and to fail to acknowledge its contradictions. Change, therefore, could only take place with change of leadership, and of outlook. The challenge was to start anew with a renewed philosophy but mirrored from the known past hat preceded the colonial era; in fact, a development which colonial imperialism interrupted.

New models of industrial and political behavior

Political philosophy that would sustain a program of industrial development after the colonial era would be broad in scope: also, it would be national and subject to national policy guidelines. The national government would be an instrument of change, initiating the process which had sometimes resulted in the disruption of the colonial order. Relationships came into being, demanding new loyalties. Independence contributed as much to defining new patterns of conduct as the advent of modern industrialization.

Two strategies to industrialization are generally considered: one based on Western models, with varying degrees of accommodation to local interests; and the other is indigenous. The literature dealing with political institutions in developing countries is already voluminous and many have tried to explain these as phenomena, quite apart from the societies which produced them, or as exercises in self-assertion. To yield to this easy temptation is to fail to see the very political structures as products of changing circumstances. Central to political conflict is the search for systems which provide the necessary dynamism for modernization. The systems chosen are neither what are needed to satisfy their wants, nor sufficiently flexible to promote full-scale modernization. While some societies are able to adapt to new conditions, others cannot and some few combine the new with the old; that is, in the process of modernizing, retain a substantial portion of tradition. Political leadership is also a factor in change. For politics is both an

index of social change and its reflection, and the
struggles that attend the politicization process are
an indication of society interacting.

Leadership and the development process

Models of modernization are incomplete without the
dynamics of leadership. Regardless of political philosophy, the process of change revolves about the
charisma of leaders to a greater degree than is generally admitted. The complexities of modern government
force them to diversify functions which increases the
bureaucracy, but it also gives more people an opportunity to become exposed to decision-making processes.
Even the most restrictive forms of government allow
more of this initiative, for any policy, however ruthless, depends on individuals for implementing and su-
pervising it. The more liberal forms of government
embrace more extensive area of citizen involvement, but
this does not imply that the degree of change is greater, or that it is more receptive to progressive influences.

Dynamic leadership consists in the ability to incorporate as many capable people as possible into positions of influence, without prejudice to the several
arms of government. Thus, one of the preoccupations
of countries emerging from the colonial era is to equip
their societies with all the paraphernalia of modernization, without sacrificing any of the gains of the immediate post-independence period.

For example, in Africa, many countries tried to
come to grips with the problem with varying degrees
of success; but largely the central question was and
still remains, how best to make available the elements
of modernization to the people without injecting the
ills that have accompanied modernization in Western
countries; how, in other words, to humanize technology
so as to minimize its deleterious effects. This was
both the stimulus and the challenge of the new political leaders in Africa, who had to fashion responses
to the new technology, or risk being engulfed by it.

Prior to initiating measures to cope with technology, leaders had to prepare the climate for change.
The transition from traditional organization to modern
could not succeed, unless it was supported by the traditional elite. In some cases pressure had to be

brought to bear to contain elements of traditional rule in the interests of national solidarity. An additional reason for moving against traditional leadership is that as their power was generally concentrated in agricultural areas, they could hamper if not actively prevent modernization. The clash of the old and the new often led to violence.

The classic example of the clash of the old and the new, traditional and modern, was the Algerian war of liberation. We are indebted to Fanon for a documentary of some of the more unsavory events that accompanied French occupation, but above all, it is his catalogue of the psychological effects of the drama on both colonizer and colonized that provides us with a background to the clash of traditional and modern, and the lessons in communication learned from this interaction. 13/

The inequities of a colonial system which had exhausted itself and run out of creative ideas, that could only perpetuate itself through oppression, brought about its own destruction. Not least among the agents that accelerated the French downfall, was the fusion of disparate elements of the Algerian people, who faced by emergency, closed ranks. The rapidity with which they were able to achieve commonality of purpose, reflected not only their overwhelming desire for freedom, but also the ability to devise communications strategy.

The rise of radio as a medium of communication between revolutionary leaders and the mass of the people was the turning point in the Algerian struggle. Radio not only was a significant logistical tool, providing much needed information about the ideology of the struggle, but also a propaganda instrument serving to educate and to encourage any wayward or flagging interest; in fact, the BBC--the British Broadcasting Corporation--performed a similar role in occupied Europe during the Second World War. But while Europeans had no need to understand the nature of the struggle against totalitarian forces, the Algerians needed to rid themselves of the colonial myth, in order to destroy it. Radio helped free the Algerian personality from confining chains of colonialism. Above all, it liberated the women, who were the most traditional element in the society. They could not be asked to fight alongside their men folk, bear arms, grenades, acts as decoys, while continuing to be

passive and subservient. The revolution changed their
role and the revolutionary tribunal was a centralized
political force that combined all the facets of a
government in operation. The assault on tradition-
alism was skilfully carried out under cover of higher
national purpose.

One aspect of modernization was accompanied without the conditions of modernization present: political
control of national resources. Models of political
communication vary, depending on differences in political organization and ideology espoused; but most rely
on the quality of leadership. Thus, the technology of
modernization depends on a number of factors and among
them: the transformation of traditional systems to be
more in tune with the needs of modern technology, leadership equal to the task and reorganization of the social structure. Even so, the proliferation of technology in the modern world has raised questions about its
impact on the individual as well as on political institutions. Technology has upset the traditional props
upon which society rests and disturbed the national
equilibrium. Carlos Fuentes suggests that this ethic,
built on a belief of continuous progress has made the
West in general insensitive to creative ideas of how
to deal with technology on humanistic terms, but it has
made it equally insensitive to values from other parts
of the world. 14/

Moreover, the overwhelming centralization which has
accompanied the introduction of technology, has confused and made more complex the discharge of the functions of government, by overwhelming bureaucracy. Government has become an assorted mass of departments
with little relationship between them and the top heavy
administration, serves mainly to delay rather than expedite solution to problems. Forms of government are
conglomerates of competing interests, espousing political programs rather than a coherent political philosophy to meet the needs of the people. Words like
liberalism, conservatism, are descriptions of attitudes
of mind, having less than precise significance in political theory or practice; and when translated become
slogans for vote-getting. Science and technology have
forced a redefinition of political ideology and the
language that supports it; yet, at the same time they
do not provide any clear indication of the direction
to be followed. This is because technology cannot
predict its path of development, hence the absence of
clues on how it should be controlled.

The influence of the West on the post-independence period was not limited to individual countries. Many of these elected to work through international organizations like the United Nations and its specialized agencies, set up for the purpose of combining moral authority with vigorous dosages of economic aid and technical assistance. Because these organizations identified the relationship between economic development and communications, they must be studied as much because of their early impact as well as because they were a conduit for Western attitudes from which technology sprung.

Notes

1/ Schiller, H. Mass Communication and American Empire. New York: Augustus M. Kelley, 1970, p. 13.

2/ Frankel, C. The Case for Modern Man. Mass.: Beacon Press, 1955.

3/ Fanon, F. Black Skins, White Masks. New York: Grove Press, 1967, p. 13.

4/ Toffler, A. Future Shock. New York: Random House, 1973.

5/ Moore, W. E. Social Change. New Jersey: Prentice Hall, 1973. The author's pradigm of social change provides much assistance in understanding the dimensions of the process.

6/ Schramm, W. Big Media, Little Media. Calif.: Stanford University Press, 1973.

7/ Ferkiss, V. The Future of Technological Civilization. New York: Braziller, 1974.

8/ Toffler, A. Op. cit., 1973.

9/ Bagdikian, B. The Information Machines. New York: Random House, 1973. The author has speculated that the year 2,000 will see three dimensional color television which would be a wholesome substitute for interpersonal meetings.

10/ Segal, R. The Race War. New York: Viking Press, 1967.

11/ Said, E. Orientalism. New York: Vintage Books, 1977. Edward Said's book provides convincing evidence how the view of the Orient was and is a product of the Western mind and invention.

12/ Oliver, R. & Fage, J. D. A Short History of Africa. London: Penguin Books, 1967.

13/ Fanon, F. The Wretched of the Earth. London: Penguin Books, 1967.

<u>14</u>/ Fuentes, C. "For the West the notion of progress replaced the notion of tragedy. With a sense of tragedy the history of the world could be understood as a conflict of equal values: Creon's spirit of order as against Antigone's spirit of freedom. Whatever the outcome, the experience was a lucid one. But once you believe that you are ordered to progress, failure becomes not tragedy but a crime. Those who oppose you are no longer equals but figures of evil. If there is one thing that is happening around the world, it is the determination of peoples not simply to accept the two versions of inevitable progress--that of Western capitalism or Soviet socialism--but to find ways of combining the power of technology with the energy of their own traditions." <u>The New York Times</u>, January 8, 1980.

Chapter 5

INTERNATIONALISM AND INFORMATION

All international organizations share a certain
mystique, derived from the positions they occupy, what
is invested in them, their theoretical objectives and
what they are trying to do in practice. And sometimes
the less precise the objectives, the more pervasive
the mystique. UNESCO is one such organization, even
though its charter is clear and its objectives defined.
The reason lies rather less in the objectives than in
the application of these objectives to education,
science and culture; and in this respect, one must
separate a general statement of principles from the
application of these principles. Herein lies the rub.

The early association of UNESCO with the communications field was accompanied by cautious enthusiasm.
First, because the practical uses of the mass media
preoccupied the resources of planners--and with good
reason, for there was much success in areas such as
literacy, dissemination of health information and so
on. Second, these uses fit into the available political systems without causing much flutter. Third,
they were successfully peddled by university establishments (governments came in much later) as acolytes of
the knowledge industry, thus disarming established
routines, which saw them as providing refuge from
constant and wearying tasks. Finally, they came predominantly from the West and were introduced with
little fanfare and trumpeting. There was no urgent
reason for worry, for the world had not yet firmly
divided along ideological grounds and new nations had
not begun to scrutinize and monitor what was designed
to assist them. And why should they? What came from
the West frequently did so in attractive packages,
promises and all, and seemed to fit into their own
developmental strategies. For example, the need to
increase basic literacy in many countries is a sine
qua non of all economic development; also, the need
for skilled personnel and adequate facilities to train
them are all self-evident goals. Radio, television
and film and other electronic technologies fit into
this general pattern.

Communication scholars and experts aided and
abetted this process by plying the new gods wherever

a forum presented itself, and it was a bold finance minister indeed, who would reject the advice of one of these consultants, recommending a spanking new radio and television station. The relationship of the United Nations, UNESCO and the merchants of industry, transnational corporations, and governments was an altogether intimate one. Both organizations represented dominant industrial interests at the international level.

Interest in the communications field as an extension of domestic hegemony tended to coexist with the efforts of the United Nations in that particular zone. The early concerns of UNESCO in the communications field show the stamp of Western interests on its deliberations and conferences. Indeed, it is not too much to say that the early history of the United Nations, like that of its predecessor, the League of Nations, bore the imprint of a Western European club. Communications was their tool for the economic, cultural and political domination of the developing world. Truman's doctrine proclaimed the economic challenge that was to quicken the pulse of American industry. 1/ The various sorties in the realm of international warfare either in defense of national interests, real or imagined, provoked or unprovoked, indulged in from 1945 to the present, contributed to the overall design. Finally, the link between economic interests, free trade, military sophistication and political acceptance ensured what some observers called the American century. 2/

But of greater significance than the role of the U.S. in the modern world is the evidence that it provides up to 40 percent of the operating budget of the United Nations and its agencies and the sobering fact of the organization's dependency and its sensitivity in the face of a threat to these funds. Its economic programs have often been threatened by cut-off of American funds: in 1971, United Nations aid was voted down by Congress soon after the United Nations vote on China. 3/ This attitude can only be explained by an identification bordering on ownership. 4/

The communications programs of the United Nations and its specialized agencies, therefore, bore an inescapable Western imprint. National development, the central focus of newly independent countries, became one of the principal recipients of attention and interest.

The timing could hardly have been more propitous. The U.S. was ready to capitalize and expand trading and other interests abroad and where it did not seek trade, pushed to its outer limits political and military ties. Western Europe, emerging from the strain of World War II, and seeking markets, eagerly embraced the opportunity for limited growth. 5/ And as the developing countries were starved of capital, technical know-how, equipment and material, the West gladly and profitably filled the vacuum. It was a movement, which as far as academia was concerned, kindled a new Renaissance of scholarship and research allied to the equally satisfying monetary rewards.

In the Western camp therefore, economic justification provided by an expansionist creed was quick to look for constitutionally sound reasons to support communication policies. To put the matter succinctly: the free movement of capital, industry, machines and men--the order of the words is deliberate--required and indeed necessitated the free flow of information. A new era of unrestrained economic growth supported by free and easy communications dawned and with it the effective dominance in such related fields as information and culture.

Significant was the intimacy of the relationship, elsewhere described, between the U.S., as moral arbiter of the Western phalanx, and the United Nations and its specialized agencies. 6/ 7/ What had started as a planned exercise, became in the process of time quite casual, as friendly satellites like the Philippines were allowed to introduce legislation in the General Assembly to support the Western position. 8/ Freedom of information was adopted internationally as a fundamental right upon which all other rights depended and that implied the right to "gather, transmit and publish news anywhere without fetters." Moreover, the United Nations Conference on Freedom of Information held in Geneva in 1948 served but to rubber stamp the early General Assembly resolution and to ensure that Freedom of Information would be foremost on the international agenda. 9/

These moves did not pass unnoticed and a certain hypocrisy characterized many of the more prominent actions in the Western camp, which, even though alive to the dangers of unchecked expansion of U.S. media power, voted for the resolution in principle. They

125

believed that the freedom principle was worthy of the
highest consideration over and above the more realis-
tic concerns of the marketplace. 10/ Thirty years
later Tunstall made a disquieting assessment of U.S.
dominion of world communications. 11/

From this period therefore dates the foundations
of that association between Western commercial interests and the United Nations and other specialized
agencies--an association based on a simple division of
the world between those that would profit most from
freedom of information and those that would not. It
is not without a certain irony that much of the debate
about the future of this division should now take place
at this level. But much water was to pass under the
bridge before this could take place. The analysis
which follows, while acknowledging specific efforts
made by the United Nations and its specialized agencies
to deal with the vexed question of information, will
discuss only general trends.

From 1969 to the present

At the close of the United Nations First Development Decade, when lack of success had become apparent,
a number of experts drew together under the aegis of
UNESCO and the Canadian National Commission in Montreal,
June 1969, to consider the "present and future role of
mass communications in society." This broad umbrella
sheltered a number of other themes, such as the impact
of mass communications on society; the present state
and organization of research; the need for research
into new fields; the need for cooperative action at the
national and international levels. The sensitive areas
dealing with the one-way flow of information and the
unbalanced flow of information were introduced, noted
and tabled for future consideration.

By then it had already been apparent to many that
this delicate subject would certainly adorn the agenda
of the international community for an indefinite time.
Behind the generalities, which tend to occupy men on
the international scene, was a genuine concern that
these issues had at long last achieved universal respectability. They had come out in the open.

Previously, the only mention was through innuendo
and the implications were lost in a mist of embarrassment. For example, Jacques Keyser's 1953 study published by UNESCO, "A Week in the World." Also, the

modern association of information and propaganda and warfare caused flow of information questions to be related in some sense to shortwave broadcasts during the Cold War period.

The final report of the Montreal Conference reflected the international agenda for the future. Under the sub-heading "Research into new fields," two important areas were identified: the first one was more usual, the second pointed to significant considerations later to bedevil the international community.

(a) News transmission as--both at the national and international levels--deserves particular attention. The news values of media practitioners should also be studied.

(b) More comprehensive, system-oriented research into mass communication is needed at all levels and in all areas. This includes the analysis of media organization, ownership and financial support, the decision-making processes in media production, the codes of professional ethics, the actual value systems of communicators, and their perception of their role in society. The special contexts of the developing countries deserve special attention. 12/

The first clause is a reaction to the increased interest of the rich industrial countries in staking out areas of interest in the developing ones and the methods used to do so. For example, radio coverage of the Voice of America, the British Broadcasting Corporation (BBC), the Deutsche Welle, the Voice of Germany, Radio Moscow, increased dramatically over the decade of the sixties. The recognition that news is inseparable from the value system of its source was acknowledged and with that the enormous possibilities of bias and the sensationalism, which often became the necessary accomplices of the process. Also, the developing countries, sensitive to the needs of their infant and growing media industry, did not wish to jeopardize them by complete reliance on foreign material. This never became more than an unfilfilled dream and today the question remains not whether they rely on foreign material but rather how much.

The second clause is the beginning of the rumblings, which later became a crescendo, about the responsibilities of the broadcaster and the need to question the motives of the messenger. Instructive is the recommendation to study "the system" at all levels and in all areas. The view circulated that communication is something more than the ways in which messages circulate, more than a hierarchical structure imposing its caveats from abroad. The experts, including university consultants as well as government representatives, implied that wider participation at the management and decision-making levels could be brought about through changes in the structure of the system.

(c) Another major problem confronting the developing nations in the field of mass communication is that, while many of them are making conscious efforts to use the media for development and are producing special programmes for this purpose, the total communication environment of these countries remains dominated by foreign-produced media content which is introducing values which are alien to their traditional cultures (para. 22).

(d) The fact that the production of mass communication materials is largely concentrated in the hands of the major developed countries also affects the role of the media in promoting international understanding. Communication at the moment is a "one-way street" and the problems of the developing nations are seen with the eyes of journalists and producers from the developed regions; moreover, the materials they produce are aimed at audiences of these regions. As a result, not only is the image of the developing nations often a fase and distorted one, but that every image is reflected back to the developing countries themselves (para. 23).

(e) The meeting felt that the international exchange of mass media content and other popular cultural artifacts in general, and particularly those which affect the developing nations, involves not only the possible displacement or modification of certain cultural values, but also the problem of mutual comprehensibility. Therefore, mass communication research is needed into the perceptual patterns peculiar to cultural and ethnic groups, which should be taken into account if international exchange of materials is not to give rise to misunderstanding. 13/ (para. 24)

These three clauses deal specifically with foreign domination of media content of developing countries. The alarm, often muted, was raised about the

128

"displacement or modification" of cultural values, which affect not only the way a country sees itself, but also is a necessary ingredient in those cherished customs and beliefs that are transmitted from one generation to another.

The concluding section deals with cooperation at the national and international levels.

(f) A practical and effective way of better study-ing and comprehending the role of mass communication on a world-wide basis is urgently required--one which would be capable of responding to a variety of problems in an efficient manner. After reviewing a number of alternative proposals, it was considered that, while both a country-by-country approach and a global ap-proach can serve some purposes, an important additional contribution will result from examining the social consequences of mass communication in a regional con-text. Many common cultural patterns and problems should be susceptible to effective analysis in this way (para. 38).

(g) The meeting therefore recommended that re-gional centres be established (or, where existing, be expanded) to promote and co-ordinate research, ensure the dissemination of research findings, and help in providing intensified programmes of training courses and seminars to encourage the exchange of views and experiences among communication researchers and prac-titioners. They should also maintain a careful and selective surveillance over major trends and develop-ments in communication research (para. 39).

(h) In addition to acting as vital links in the exchange of research and training activities at the national levels, the regional centres should also be-come the basis for wider international integration of knowledge about mass communication (para. 40). 14/

The Montreal conference of experts on mass com-munication and society is important for two reasons. It was the first demonstrated awareness of a growing problem, amid a comfortable alliance of private, pub-lic, government and non-governmental participants and observers. Second, its recommendations set the stage for much of the work that was to occupy the interna-tional community in the decade that followed. Indeed,

129

its challenge to the world community to research issues of mass communication and society from interdisciplinary approaches spawned a movement that was to unite the theorists as well as practitioners and others in critical but committed ways.

Of importance is the definition of UNESCO's role as one of "leadership" (my italics), encouragement and liaison. As the decade progressed much of the subsequent criticism of that organization's role failed to consider how it defined itself and what its proper functioning is in regard to these matters.

It seemed increasingly clear that when UNESCO chose actively to exercise its rights to leadership, it offended those interests that wished passive maintenance of the status quo. Criticism is hushed when piecemeal change is involved, but when its exertions become more substantive, protests of alarm fill the air.

While the Montreal conference identified the main problems that were to later divide the international community, it was not until much later that the full impact began to be felt. Furthermore, the gradual involvement of UNESCO in education and cultural activities in many of the developing countries, seemed to pave the way for more conspicuous political involvement. In a sense the field was wide open. Countries which were eager for development aid from whatever quarter it came, did not mind international assistance from an organization which appeared non-ideological and which had the reputation of a friendly tribunal.

Many conferences had been taking place before Montreal and those at Bangkok (1960), Chile (1961), Paris (1962) and Tunisia (1963) attempted to remedy both inadequate information channels and to develop information agencies. Typical of the reports issued was that on information channels in Latin America.

The meeting noted that although the mass media were, on the whole, more considerably developed in Latin America than in South East Asia or Africa, there were few national news agencies in the region.

...Equally, a free flow of information on technical, scientific and cultural advances was essential as a means of helping the Latin American peoples to carry out their programmes of economic development. The initiative in achieving this objective, it was felt, must come from the Latin American peoples themselves. 15/

UNESCO grew in stature as broker in mass communications and Under-Secretary-General Maheu outlined a Long-Term Plan (1971-76), which was to serve as a working guideline for that organization's later policies, with the emphasis on content rather than techniques. What promoted this enhanced interest in the field were the new "fears and promises" of Space broadcasting. There is convincing evidence of this in many reports on Space Communication, culminating in the Draft Declaration on the Use of Outer Space. In fact, UNESCO had put out a publication, Communication in the Space Age, in which a stable of its favorite consultants had almost euphorically pointed to the possibilities in Outer Space, even as they outlined some of the difficulties:

> "The central fact at present is that technological developments are far outrunning the economic and political developments that must occur before the new technology can come into wide use..." 16/

The free flow of information

Communication in Outer Space underlined the question of the free flow of information that had become an issue during the Cold War and the use of shortwave radio for propaganda purposes. It was evident that a country that had extensive communication facilities at its disposal, could be at a considerable advantage.

Countries of Eastern Europe in their continued battle with Radio Free Europe, Radio Liberty and Radio in the American Sector of Berlin (RIAS), recognized this. Thus, the allied reflections of television technology, and the role of the brokers of international media traffic came in for special study. For example, "Television Traffic--a one-way street," "External Broadcasting and International Understanding," "International News Agency Traffic," and "The Role of the Multinationals in the Distribution of Film and Television Materials." 17/

131

It was not only developments in space that concerned UNESCO. Space technology was a part of the amazing progress made in telecommunications, leading to increase in international communication and proliferation of informational, educational and cultural materials. World communications networks provide the opportunity for instant exchange of news and features; and the growth of informational channels stimulated the expansion of news agency services the world over. The growth of these services helped regional groupings to share cultural experiences in Europe, for example, while others, namely, the Arab States, Asia and Latin America, started to do the same.

UNESCO was still worried about the magnitude of the problems and especially the information imbalance. Despite the technical strides made, a large part of the world continued to suffer from lack of information and means for the transmission of news and ideas. In fact, World Communications showed the large gaps among some Member States in basic information and just how poorly served Africa and a large part of Asia were. 18/ Equally disturbing, too, was an information imbalance within these countries, which favored the city dweller over the country; and where television existed, it was confined mainly to the city areas.

If the flow of information was essentially an urban phenomenon within most of Africa and Asia, it was just as heavily imbalanced between countries. For example, information flowed from the industrialized countries to the developing ones in the form of television programming, book production, and other assorted material, including entertainment fare. Statistics of the time showed what was not surprising to many; namely, that 75 percent of the content of television programs came from North America and 80 percent of the book production is done by 30 industrialized countries, compared to 20 percent produced in the developing countries, from which 70 percent of the world population comes. 19/

But figures don't tell the whole story by any means. They do not speak to the prominence of the multinational corporations that dictate and preside over these commercial dealings; and while they transfer much needed technical knowledge, do so in a manner that evokes challenges of cultural imperialism and technological dependence.

132

"While, on the one hand, the importance of
the free flow of information is widely accepted as the basis of mutual understanding,
many developing countries are concerned
that their lack of communication facilities deny them the opportunity of informing the world of their problems, aspirations, and contribution to the culture of
mankind. At the same time, the fact that
they are the recipients of a disproportionate volume of information and entertainment
from foreign sources leaves them concerned
about the preservation of their own cultural integrity and system of values. The
future possibility of direct broadcasts
via satellites has intensified this concern." 20/

The concerns that UNESCO addressed were by no
means idle. Newly independent countries, sensitive
about the poverty of their information resources, were
reluctant to admit those of others, which they saw as
threatening. UNESCO during this period did not see its
role as defender of the emerging majority of developing countries. Rather, that organization tried to define itself as arbiter of a problem that was later to
become quite controversial. It tried to develop principles that could provide some comfort for both contending parties--the rich industrialized countries and
the developing ones. Principles after all could have
universal validity, and duties and responsibilities
could be extended to institutions and individuals
alike.

At the core of UNESCO's motives was the belief in
the importance of communication and the information
flow to developing countries in the process of building new societies frequently on shaky foundations. It
came to be realized that if political independence was
to be more than empty rhetoric, a determined and vigorous assault had to be made on the many problems they
faced. Access to information through communications
media would be a necessary first step to achieve a yet
distant objective. Access and communication strategies are incomplete without other fundamental considerations, such as the rethinking of "ideologies" associated with information. Inevitably, the view
gained credence that information could not take place
in an ideological vacuum, that information necessarily

133

took on the contours of the system within which it operated. Developing countries were in the process of reexamining that system and questioning the underlying realities upon which it is based.

Ideology and communication

Familiar definitions came under relentless scrutiny and customary meaning translated into political terminology. Words such as "free," stripped of philosophical nicety, became the target of searching analysis. A close parallel exists in the world of technology, which insists on going beyond the comfortable world of the usual and constantly seeks "to exceed its grasp...or what's a heaven for." Similarly, Third World countries seek to reach out beyond the accepted definitions of "freedom," access and participation to embrace forms of communication, which though controversial, they would embrace all the same.

Moreover, these countries saw in an expanded communication system the means for greater citizen participation and support for the decision-making process at all levels. 21/

UNESCO's reaction to this break in tradition was to seek first to understand it, then next to place it in some philosophical context.

It has always been part of Western tradition to construct a viable theory around what is new as a prelude to understanding it, or to aid understanding, and also to construct a theory about what is not properly understood in order to mythicize it.

This tradition that had so faithfully served the international community had impeccable credentials: it had the benediction of Article 19 of the Universal Declaration of Human Rights and the support and allegiance of influential members of the international community led by the U.S.

Right to communicate

This emerging idea spelled doom of freedom of information and is a response to several factors: an increasing awareness of the role of communication in society and of its importance in securing or endangering the life of individuals; the immense scientific and technological progress; the awakening of the Third World; and the maturing recognition of the interdependence of societies and countries. 22/

In order for this to be understood, it had first to be broken down into specific areas, each of which appears to have its own terminology and reference. For example, a tentative chronology might read: the Right to Communicate; specific communication rights; communication issues; communication environment.

The right to communicate concept has the doubtful advantage of being all things to all men: to government, it promises an understanding relationship with the media, or at least a relationship of some sort; to citizens, it appears that their voices would be heard by those in power, even though responses may not always be immediately forthcoming, or forthcoming; to private media, it suggests that they would be allowed to operate in a friendlier atmosphere than hitherto, and that the climate of animosity, which so often affects news dissemination would be at an end; to all information sources it holds out the olive branch and a defense of their rights to participate in the State; to other institutions and organizations it does likewise; to States it holds out the genuine promise of the ebb and flow of communication in an environment that is conducive to it; and to the individual it defends his right to seek and to exchange information, and the protection of his personal viewpoints. Indeed, the right to communicate conceot touches the whole State, which would be expected to honor and defend its rights and responsibilities within the international community.

UNESCO and the right to communicate

UNESCO became most interested in the new concept for three reasons basically: first, because that organization had been disappointed at the narrow focus of the First Development Decade which, despite the loftiness of its ideals and pronouncements, came woefully short of reaching them; second, "it was becoming a matter of urgency for the developing countries to establish a communications infrastructure able to cover urban and rural zones alike and accessible to all social classes;" 23/ third, because "the strategy adopted for the Second Development Decade starting January 1971, in the view of UNESCO, failed adequately

135

to deal with the contribution of media of communication to development." 24/ For example, media were limited to public relations functions among those countries that had a development program for human resources and the mass society; and propaganda functions, where they were associated with a dominant ideology. Developed and developing countries shared this common view of mass media functions. Both public relations and propaganda functions were related to public objectives, but there was nothing inherent in either to cause one to assume that the public would be able to speak freely.

The mass media had taken on distinct roles, one of which was setting the public agenda and the other was helping to improve the quality of life. The full participation of people, particularly in the developing countries, was necessary to achieve these ends. In the more advanced industrialized countries, the mass media provided rich and continuing opportunities for personal enrichment and contribution.

Indeed, Development Support Communication, designed to enlist the help of agencies within these countries, to promote their own development, was a step in this direction. But this was no substitute for planned policy and comprehensive development of the field of communication. Moreover, there was need for planned policy, not least because of the many agencies, which were becoming part of the general act: the Agency for International Development (AID), the Canadian International Development Agency (CIDA), were two apart from the specialized agencies of the United Nations. A concerted and focused effort could pay dividends, even though motives might be dissimilar.

Accordingly, UNESCO made the first tentative approach to creating policy for the mass media, policy based on research and a methodology "for the application of the new 'community' technologies with the principal aim of opening access to the media systems." 25/ These strategies were in fact the beginning of the national communication policies that were to be so significant in the organization's future direction for the Third World.

National communication policies must be seen against the background of the right to communicate, which began to occupy the energies of the organization along with that of scholars and governments. Indeed, the right to communicate provided a means of abandoning the freedom of information concept in the absolute and doctrinaire sense, and broadening the basis of the communication process. Central to this view was the new Director General of UNESCO, M'Bow, who reflected much of that organization's policies, when he referred to the interrelation of the major issues facing humanity, of which "the new international economic order" was prominent:

> "The new awareness of the role of communication as an indispensable element of all social organization, has resulted in interest in aspects of the communication processes which previously have not been taken into account. 26/

UNESCO recognized the broad possibilities in the right to communicate to challenge the established and hallowed system of freedom of information. But possibilities are one thing; it was quite another matter to obtain the approval or agreement for them. New concepts are difficult to define and the right to communicate seemed especially so, even though it has a familiar and obvious ring to it.

Some of the questions it poses are: is this right an individual right? Is it a collective right? If it is a collective right, to what extent is the collective (i.e., for example, the government) subject to sanctions. If there are sanctions, what kind of sanctions must there be and who will impose them? Since freedom of the press is subject to ethical standards and not punitive sanctions, would the same apply to a government which insists on active participation in the information field?

The whole issue of press freedom therefore was for a time circumvented and the main thrust became the right to communicate. It may have been fondly hoped by UNESCO that the issue of press freedom was not as vital to the more compelling problems of national economic development in the Third World. Also, UNESCO, through the Director General, may have believed that once the world community agreed at the Eighteenth General Conference (1976) to study the right to communicate and related issues, press freedom might be seen as marginal to the whole rather than the whole itself. But the reverse seemed to occur. Press freedom became and still is the major issue upon which all others depend and the right to communicate, although a major point of discussion is cloistered in the halls of academy and the subject of vigorous debate at various United Nations related seminars.

The focal point of this right is the view that countries must and should have the same right as individuals to receive and impart information.

Third World countries are the foci of much of the ideology of the right to communicate and the New International Information Order is a response to the one-way flow of information that has been an essential part of the dependency relationship, with the rich industrial countries, and the transnational corporations. The right to communicate escapes precise definition and it may well be that a suitable one is not possible--definition outside of a particular socio-political and cultural environment is incomplete. But the New International Information Order, which will be later examined, emerged as a practical consideration in place of the elusive right to communicate.

The idea was the brainchild of Jean d'Arcy, Director of Radio and Visual Services in the Office of Public Information at the United Nations, who wrote "the time will come when the Universal Declaration of Human Rights will have to encompass a more exclusive right than man's right to information, first laid down twenty-one years ago in Article 19. This is the right of man to communicate." 27/ But d'Arcy could not anticipate the swift developments in technology which, within years could place a man on the moon and expand the boundaries of the communications field to include broadcast satellites, computers, and videotape recorders. Human responses have lagged behind this technological prowess.

Communication policy has been initiated in many countries as a means of channelling communication needs and services through guidelines and rules. But no one can be sure that these guidelines are effective, or that they enable all citizens to share in the right to communicate equally. Indeed, the application of technology (and the establishment of unnecessary television stations in Africa and Latin America is part of this) did not in any way guarantee that people were prepared to act any swifter to messages from governing administrations; or, that the latter enjoyed the confidence of the people because of its enhanced ability to communicate.

Thus UNESCO found itself facing the dilemma of supporting a right which could not be defined to everyone's satisfaction; and, even if defined, could not guarantee the effective rights enshrined in Article 19 of the Universal Declaration of Human Rights.

But despite its limitations, this right did imply that the one-way flow of information that was so exclusive, could not remain so any longer in a world where future technological and other developments increased both the flow of international news and well as global interdependence.

UNESCO and Member States

UNESCO continues to move in the direction of interpreting the policies of member states. If at times that organization has seemed to be in the vanguard of and for change, it is because of an inherited idealism. If it has seemed to side less with the established countries, it is because it has perceived the changing realities of world conditions necessitate that change. And if the right to communicate challenges the sacred cows of the established, it is proper for them to examine the reasons why it does. Evidence of the storm created by the implications of the right to communicate is readily seen in UNESCO conferences at Bogota, Quito and Nairobi.

Reasons for much of the hubbub are not difficult to discover. International relations have until now been defined by the rich and powerful countries. They have demarcated those areas which are privileged and those which are not. They have decided what should constitute the international agenda. Likewise they have defined the fate of regimes and with casual reference to professed standards, supported those which operated in their own best interests: and in Iran the U.S. utilized the mass media to throw invective on a revolution which it did not fully understand. 28/ Lest it be forgotten, a particularly aggressive form of internationalism divided Africa at the Treaty of Berlin in 1873, and invaded and occupied Abbysinia in 1933.

The emergence of the Third World disturbed the foundations of the international establishment. What has to be admitted is precisely that which is most

139

worth defending: the familiar world view which sanctioned the rule of the rich over the poor, and conventional political systems over the eclectic, ethnocen-
tricity over multiculture. UNESCO conferences at
Bogota, Quito, San Jose (Costa Rica) and Nairobi, among
others, are evidence of the struggle of the established
order to cope with a changing world.

The writing on the wall

These new realities were obvious from the start.
The 1974 Bogota meeting was considered as a preparation
for the intergovernmental conference of the following
year. This meeting was heavily political as the agenda
indicated:

- The ideological context of communication policy: role of the state in the
  formulation of a national, coherent
  and corrective policy;

- The difficulty of applying a national
  communication policy without the participation of the government and institutions;

- Creation of National Communication Coun-
  cils; and

- The role of UNESCO in the communication
  sector and the objectives of national
  and international cooperation. 29/

Prior to the Bogota conference, a significant
event was the Fourth Conference of Heads of State or
Government of Non-Aligned Countries in Algiers, 1973,
where much attention was drawn to the "...obnoxious
effect of the way in which the mass media of the industrialized world have developed their markets within the framework of the principles of the free flow
of information." 30/ This observation led the non-
aligned countries, a part of which was made up of Third
World representatives, to promote a greater interchange
of ideas among themselves:

To reorganize existing communication channels which are the legacy of the colonial
past and which have hampered free, direct
and fast communication between them,

140

To initiate action for the revision of existing multilateral agreements with a view to reviewing press cable rates and facilitating faster and cheaper intercommunication,

To take urgent steps to expedite the process of collective ownership of communication satellites and evolve a code of conduct for directing their use, and

To promote increased contact between the mass media, universities, libraries, planning and research bodies and other institutions so as to enable developing countries to change experience and share ideas. 31/

The experts assembled at Bogota were given to the trumpeting of much ideology, and communication policy reflected this. For example, communication policies are inseparable from an ideological framework; a communication system must be linked to the objectives of a development policy. This underlined the shift in UNESCO's conceptual strategies for the role of communications in Third World countries. It is especially significant that the site of the meeting of experts was in Latin America, which was and is the focus of so much of the imperial energies of the U.S. 32/ It was this which forced a policy shift by UNESCO.

The need for political, economic and cultural independence is forcing member states of the region to assume overall control over their national mass communication policy, a control which has hitherto been exercised partly by practice, by private cultural enterprise. 33/

Privately owned media had not, it must be admitted, a good record of citizen participation in Latin America, and the mass media have not been over eager to open doors to the public. In fact, the consumer movement in the U.S., in addition to various citizen lobbies (the National Organization for Women, B'nai Brith, Black Efforts for Soul in Television, Action for Children's Television), have been in the vanguard, among others, demanding greater sensitivity by the major networks to the public business. 34/ This is in sharp contrast to the Federal Communication

Commission (FCC) which has sought with doubtful success
to cajole the television networks into doing the public's business. 35/

The report of the experts was therefore a departure from the usual and as Latin America was in the midst
of a new development decade, it seemed all the more
necessary to depart from the established forms of communication behavior and try new approaches. Though un-
pleasant, they were, in fact, more than common sense
suggestions in a continent where the failure to communicate and the inability to encourage even the semblance
of social communication was "honored more in the breach
than in the observance."

Access, which is "the extent to which people can
send and receive messages through the media" and participation, which is "the exercise of the right...to
take part in the making of decisions as to the planning,
use and control of the communications media," can therefore be understood as aspects of the communications problem addressed; namely, the failure of people to mean-
ingfully participate in the affairs of their country.
Because of this, a national communications policy was
recommended; and with regard to privately owned media,
the conference agreed to "impose certain services and
programs, thus controlling their operations as regards
messages, content and the frequency of advertising
etc." 36/

The total effect of these recommendations was to
broaden the idea of freedom of expression, by making it
more the rights of the community, than the exclusive
prerogative of the idols of the market place.

What appeared to be then but a tentative approach
to communications problems, assumed an altogether more
formal appearance at the UNESCO-sponsored meeting on
the development of news exchange at Quito, June 1975.
As far as general discussion can provide significant
clues to the pulse of international conferences, it
was evident that the conclusions of the Bogota meeting
were the basis of much of the deliberations.

"...news exchanges of the kind in question
should proceed from the basic consideration
that communication is a public service. It
was therefore essential that the States of
the region should take part in them. 37/

142

"Also...an optimum and equitable flow of news
and information was needed among the countries of the Latin American and Caribbean region, in order to safeguard its sovereignty
and to foster development of national identity and regional awareness." 38/

Both the Bogota and the Quito meetings indicate
that UNESCO came out firmly on the side of national
communications policies. Information was acknowledged
as a means of emphasizing national identity, and of
shoring it up where it was in danger of disappearance,
or threatened with disappearance. That information
policies should be in harmony with the national development plans of governing administrations cannot be
denied.

But UNESCO was not prime mover. The organization
did not assemble a bunch of scholars and other interested parties to rubber stamp its proposals. Rather,
it seemed that UNESCO was encouraged by the general
trend of the submitted papers and tone of the discussion to implement strategies for national communication
policies. In addition, many countries in the region
had themselves been moving in that direction prior to
both Bogota and Quito. A number of them, such as
Brazil, Argentina and Peru, had already set up the
structural machinery for government participation in
the mass media long before UNESCO convened meetings to
discuss the subject. And the shortcomings of the system had long been common knowedge to most of them. The
only difference now was that a self-conscious nationalism had found expression in new ways of tackling an
old problem.

UNESCO was not neutral in these deliberations.
It was both arbiter and practitioner of its own cause.
To deny that information imbalance had become a subject
of importance, it could not do. To deny that the realities of world information favored the rich at the expense of the poor, would have been to mock the intelligence. But by acknowledging the problem and attending
it, UNESCO could work towards a rapprochement with the
rich nations, which had become anxious about their en-
trenched privileges.

The establishment of regional news agencies in
the Latin American and Caribbean regions appeared to
threaten the monopoly of existing news agencies such

as Reuters, Associated Press and United Press International, although neither of these agencies made a tremendous profit from the region. 39/ Two recommendations of the Quito conference speak expressly to this.

(j) The establishment of national news agencies will afford a suitable basis for the subsequent creation of a large-scale Latin American and Caribbean agency...

(k) It is recommended that the respective governments take the necessary steps to avoid the distortion of news that is so frequent on the part of international agencies. 40/

Much has been made of "the conflict between such purposeful social engineering and the individual's rights to choose;" and it has been pointed out that the latter was not high on the priority of the majority of those present. But this is to imply that the individual's right to choose is as staunch as a birthright and not subject to the vagaries of fortune, beyond the machinations of all governments, or the collective thrust of all cultural and social phenomena. 41/

Bogota and Quito were preparatory meetings for the Intergovernmental Conference on Communications and Policies in San Jose, Costa Rica, July 1976. This conference was marked by the opposition of the Inter-American Press Association and the Inter-American Broadcasters' Association, which viewed the agenda as contrary to UNESCO's own constitution. The conference was noteworthy for the 30 recommendations that reinforced the prevailing beliefs that the role of governments in communications policies should be enlarged. Widely ranging and ambitious, the recommendations sought to combine ideas for a "more balanced international circulation and communication," with the bureaucratic machinery for carrying it out within Latin America and the Caribbean. This region had become a "test case" for the efforts to link communication agencies; that is, news agencies with vigorous local attempts to assert national identity. Governments were held responsible for preserving this balance.

Often omitted by the critics of the Costa Rica conference was the responsibility attached to governments to guarantee the rights of freedom of expression, access and participation of all media within their respective countries; in effect, to guarantee the right to communicate. UNESCO itself pledged "to take steps

as soon as possible to hold meetings of legal, professional and scientific experts in communication for
the purpose of providing a legal definition and struc-
turing of the principles of the right to communicate." 42/

Government guarantees, it might be argued, are not
worth much in the absence of a specific willingness to
do so, but they do at least establish a legal framework.
All constitutions depend finally on the willingness and
integrity of these in whose interests they are framed.

Much importance was attached within the region to
the training personnel, the establishment of a regional centre, dissemination of "low cost radio and television receivers, as well as film, newspapers and
other hardware necessary for effective social communication, communication research and training; satellites
and the development of regional policy with regard to
them.

UNESCO, on the other hand, was requested to promote the development of communication and "a balanced
relationship in the international flow of information
and communication."

The Costa Rica conference was in some respects a
watershed. In it UNESCO came out firmly and unequivo-
cably on the side of a Third World region (Latin America
and the Caribbean), that was not noted for either the
sophistication of its technology, or the abilities of
communication channels to reach themasses of people.

Criticism of UNESCO

UNESCO's commitment is seen by many as a political
act, not in keeping with its charter. Also, its firm
advocacy of national communications policies, support
of government-owned media, encouragement of local news
agencies and a "wholistic" view of the communications
process, brought about a not inconsiderable concern
in circles pledged to the pursuit of "objective truth
as a guide" to international conduct. 43/ 44/

But the proponents of this idealism, omit the
historical record of national organizations in the
international arena, where cut and thrust continue
unabatedly; 45/ and the World Radio Conference and the
struggle for radio frequencies is the most recent example of it.

UNESCO is at the forefront of the battle for communications policies and relations with the established
order, as properly it should be. If it is "political,"
the organization but reflects the inclinations of member states and the realities of the hour. That some of
its pronouncements has been obtuse and downright un-
pleasant (the resolution linking zionism with racism,
for instance), and deeply disturbing, should not de-
flect from the value of its work.

UNESCO is not the "voice" of the Third World, but
reflects the numerical strength of member states. What
the delegates from member states did at Costa Rica was
supped up by M'Bow, Secretary-General of UNESCO:

> "...that undiscerning acceptance of the
> free flow of information in a world,
> which is dominated by economic inequal-
> ity runs counter to the generous inten-
> tions which these principles purport to
> serve. Their unthinking application
> amounts in practice to granting de facto
> monopolies to the most powerful communi-
> cators in the international communi-
> ty." 46/

The response of the established powers was not long in
coming. The historic nineteenth General Conference
in Nairobi was the battleground of conflicting views.

The Nairobi watershed

Nairobi is important for it represented a major
platform of conflicting ideologies. Article XII of
the Soviet draft declaration 19C/91 on the "use of the
mass media" provided grist for the mill; the resolution intended the press to be subservient to the
government. Without assessing the merits or demerits
of the Soviet Union's position, it was clear that this
represented a challenge to UNESCO in two respects.

It was the first General Conference held in Africa,
and the first African Director-General of the organization, and there was some pressure on M'Bow, the
Director-General, for a successful conclusion to its
deliberations. Second, UNESCO faced in no uncertain
way the threat of U.S. withdrawal of funds, amounting
to 25 percent of the total allotment.

The Western response to the Soviet draft resolution was predictable: the resolution posed a threat to the Universal Declaration of Human Rights, which guaranteed freedom of expression and the freee flow of information. UNESCO thus found itself in the middle of an East-West conflict that was reminiscent of the Cold War period.

What could it do? A procedural arrangement allowed the organization to postpone consideration, while steps were taken to seek a compromise of some sort. Thus the West's position forced UNESCO into the position of arbiter between East and West. And it was well that it should be at the center of the debate, for the main thrust of that organization's policies up to Nairobi was not inconsistent with government access and participation in the communications field, but totally inconsistent with government control. The Soviet draft resolution therefore was both in letter and spirit against the policy of UNESCO.

Nevertheless, much was salvaged at Nairobi; a program for the promotion of the free and balanced flow of information; research on the role of communication in society; and an undertaking to assist member states in the formulation and implementation of national policies were part of the limited though worthwhile achievements. The Draft Declaration had, however, raised serious and difficult questions, and while compromise was strategic, it could not indefinitely postpone the inevitable battlefield of opinions.

Accordingly, "a review of the totality of the problems of communication in modern society," seemed a logical step for determining "the problems which call for fresh action at the national level and a concerted, overall approach at the international level. Also, the review was to include "attention to the problems relating to the free and balanced flow of information in the world, as well as the specific needs of developing countries." Finally,

> to define the role which communication
> might play in making public opinion aware
> of the major problems besetting the world,
> in sensitizing it to these problems and
> helping gradually to solve them by con-
> cerned action at the national and interna-
> tional levels.

Eventually, the controversial "Draft Declaration of fundamental principles concerning the contribution of the mass media to strengthening peace and international understanding, the promotion of human rights and to countering racialism, apartheid and incitement to war," was approved at the Twentieth General Conference in Paris, 1978. Some of its provisions are worth examining.

The two troublesome spots in the original draft had to do with access and participation, both of which had the draft been passed as it was, would have given governments the right to control the mass media within their respective states and a freedom to dispose of the mass media as they wished.

The approved draft neatly sidestepped both areas, which presumably is the aim of compromise, and adopted a stance, which, while not specifically denying governments the right to have their say, does not give them outright permission to control the media.

> "Access by the public to information should be guaranteed by the diversity of the sources and means of information available to it...Similarly, it is important that the mass media be responsible to concerns of peoples and individuals, thus promoting the participation of the public in the elaboration of information."

The Third World was satisfied that Article VI of the revised draft went far in the direction of acknowledging one of their most serious complaints; namely, that the old information order discriminated against them:

> "For the establishment of a new equilibrium and greater reciprocity in the flow of information, which will be conducive to the institution of a just and lasting peace and to the economic and political independence of the developing countries, it is necessary to correct the inequalities in the flow of information to and from developing countries, and between these countries."

148

At the same time Article IX invited the developed countries "to contribute to the creation of the conditions for a free flow and wider and more balanced dissemination of information...," an "invitation," which under the circumstances of their previous concerns, could not be balked at. Nor could they object to Article X, which counselled how important it was "that a free flow and wider and better balanced dissemination of information be encouraged."

The Declaration also challenged the developed countries, the possessors of sophisticated technology, "to facilitate the procurement by the mass media in the developing countries, of adequate conditions and resources enabling them to gain strength and expand..." Thus clause 3 within Article X was taken to refer to such advanced technology capability as satellites, which several of the Third World countries were becoming interested and indeed involved in, notably India.

The Declaration clearly did not measure up to everyone's ideas, but could it? Third World countries were reasonably satisfied; indeed, the Declaration could be said to have done more for them than the developed countries. They stood to gain access to technology, and the more demanding of their governments could see in the Declaration an invitation for greater access to the channels of communication without guilt.

The developed world obtained what they sought: a Declaration which expressly denied government control, which had sufficient guarantees for freedom of expression as not to perturb their conscience or their capital. Above all, it indicated to them that in the East-West confrontation they had succeeded in thwarting the influence of the Soviet Union. The challenge to them to facilitate procurement of adequate resources by the developing countries, was a small exchange for the principles of freedom they so vigorously defended. In any case, the transfer of technology benefitted them as well, for development aid conditions ensured that help of any sort was to be purchased at a price.

Again, for the Third World, the Draft Declaration went a considerable way in supporting their moral opprobrium against racialism, apartheid, and oppression.

"...mass media through the world, by reason of their role, contribute effectively to promoting human rights, in particular by giving expression to oppressed peoples who struggle against colonialism, neo-colonialism, foreign occupation and all forms of racial discrimination and oppression and who are unable to make their voices heard within their own countries."

Granted that this theoretical expression of an ethical problem would be difficult to administer, still, it shared the same fate of all codes of ethics: its application depended on the voluntary goodwill of media practitioners and the support received from public opinion and government. Ethical codes seldom have universal applicability.

Also, the omission of the controversial Article XIII of the original Draft presented at Nairobi, which gave states the rights of the mass media within their province, and the omission of the equally controversial and damaging resolution equating Zionism with racialism, did much to redeem a document which, despite its many theoretical and high-sounding phrases is bland.

The opponents of the Draft Resolution believe that it is poisonous for freedom of the press. What is more, they assert that UNESCO's continuing support of national and international communications policies are a balm and encouragement to some governments to control the mass media generally, and to initiate legislation specifically to smother them.

There is always a likelihood of government imposing curbs on the mass media for motives, which though morally defensible, might strike the impartial observer as impure. For example, the latest in a succession of cases involving the press in the U.S. and the Supreme Court gives pause. Indeed, these dealings were the principal concerns of the American Society of Newspaper Editors meeting in the nation's capital in April 1980.

Free press on trial

In the U.S. many reporters and editors were worried about the effects of the Supreme Court rulings with regard to newsroom searches, access to judicial

150

proceedings and libel. They had the uneasy feeling
that the effect of these rulings would muzzle press
coverage of government corruption in general. The
Supreme Court, seemed bent on reversing the triumphs
of Watergate, which could not happen at the present
moment, given the effect of these court decisions,
even if the press wished it. In general, these court
decisions have had a very definite dampening effect
on our aggressive pursuit in some areas," William F.
Thomas, editor of the Los Angeles Times. 47/ (See
Appendix IV for further discussion.)

Not the press alone has been subject to interpre-
tations of law by the U.S. Supreme Court. In Herbert
v. Lando, the Supreme Court held that a public figure
who sued for libel, had the right to ask questions in
pretrial discovery about the thoughts, opinions and
conclusions of the reporter who had prepared the article (in this case a broadcast). The net effect of
these court decisions can be seen in newsroom practices
"which would have been unheard of a few years ago, including formal procedures for destroying notes or
transferring them to an officer of the news organization; the issuance of wallet-sized cards to reporters
with statements to be read aloud in court stating the
news organization's objection in the event a judge
bars the press from the courtroom." 48/

In England, the condition of the press is all but
well and the ambiguity of its relations with the public
and proprietors, is secondary only to the hypocrisy of
admitting that a liberal free press theory still persists. Concentration of ownership and monopoly destroyed the foundations of a free newspaper market,
both at the national and provincial levels. And the
continuing debate about government subsidy of the
press flies in the face of the liberal ideology, which
would separate government from press altogether. Furthermore, the definition of the freedom of the press
by the Royal Commission on the Press (1977:8-9) clearly shows that freedom is in the interests of proprietors:

"We define the freedom of the press as that
freedom from restraint which is essential
to enable proprietors, editors and journalists to advance the public interest by
publishing the facts and opinions without
which a democratic electorate cannot make
responsible judgments." 49/

A 'constitutional' working example of this definition stands out in the proposals for a free press
charter. "All seven clauses in its proposed charter
detail 'essential safeguards' for press freedom pre-
venting the principal organization representing the
people, who write newspapers from exercising any influence on the contents of the press." 50/ In brief,
the interests of publishers are more important than
the reporters and journalists.

Press freedom is subject to the realities of corporate finance, technological efficiency, and ideological niceties everywhere. To attack the Draft Declaration because it does not subscribe to ideological
"purity" is unfair, the more so as the brunt of this
criticism comes from those countries that even now
are experiencing a not inconsiderable social and legal
confusion.

Furthermore, among the criticisms levelled at
UNESCO is that it is in the forefront of ideological
stances which are irreconciliable "because they concern the relationship of government to society, and
the individual to government." 51/ The ideological
positions represented by government on the one hand
and the press on the other are irreconciliable and
mutually exclusive. The job of the press in the traditional sense of the freedom of the press is literally to be free and independent of such interests as
would prevent it from exercising its rights to inform
and also to act as a critic of government. Thus, the
function of the press is quite different to the function of the government; where their interests do col-
lide might be at the point where they share the same
views of and about the citizen and his welfare.

UNESCO is not the only supra governmental organization that has tried to bridge the gap between government and society. In fact, increasingly some governments have dared to try to accommodate a failing press
by providing subsidies or redistributive schemes, thus
reconciling "liberal theory with reality by attempting
running repairs on the 'free market' designed to make
it operate more in the way that it is supposed to in
theory." 52/

But to aid the press to operate on sound financial
bases is not to participate in its ideology and certainly many of these governments (like that of West

Germany's, for example) would argue that government subsidy has not diminished the vigor and ardor of press criticism. Thus, ideological positions are irreconciliable not because they concern the relationship of government to society. They are irreconciliable because there is an unwillingness to conceive of that possibility.

This is not to imply that the status quo should continue to exist unchallenged, or that UNESCO should cease to refine its policies and programs; rather, there should be a greater commitment to do so as the organization is now held accountable for much of its global performance by critics who would wish it to support the continued mass media dominance by the West.

UNESCO and internationalism

But it is clear that the course of internationalism, so vigorously criticized by some when it goes against national interests, and so defended when it is in accord with national interests, must proceed. It must proceed because the consequence of an end or a diversion from statutory internationalism would be a disaster, paving the way for unchecked, undiluted and unrestrained nationalism. The same critics that would now wish an end to UNESCO's ideological stance in communications, forget that UNESCO has always been ideological. Indeed, its very foundation was in response to an ideological position, deriving from the conviction that a responsible internationalism could divert the world from all too rampant national energies. Moreover, the free flow of information concept that dominated the early history of the organization was an ideology hewn, carved and formed from the history and philosophy of the West. How then could these critics wish to have an ideology-free organization?

UNESCO is called upon to act as honest broker in a world in which now 161 Member States compete with unequal voices, but with equal vigor, for their right to be heard. Information with its sharp ideological perspectives has divided the organization in three principal areas: first, the member states, led by the U.S. support the free flow of information; second, those countries which support government control of information; finally, those countries that wish to see governments share access to the communications media.

These views often are in sharp contrast and conflict.

Not least of the problems that UNESCO has had to
face was that germinated by the East-West conflict
between the Soviet Union and the United States. To
this, add the emergence of the Third World and its
insistence on the participatory role of governments
in the information business and the picture is complete. UNESCO has had to adapt to these shifting and
often teacherous sands, in which information (what
the issue appears to be about) is often secondary to
the power and sensitivity of the great powers. The
1976 Nairobi conference, for instance, brought the
defeat of the Soviet Union's call for control of information. That conference also indicated that the
Third World seemed to be more concerned with access
to communication outlets than information control--a
view which underlined the Third World's unwillingness
to moderation and compromise.

The conference on Security and Cooperation (CSCE),
in Helsinki, 1975, was a battlefield for these views.
The Soviet Union, while acknowledging that information
dissemination was a fit subject for international concern, nevertheless advanced the views that the State
has the right to disseminate information within its
midst. Thus, the free exchange of information once
again became the subject of national interpretation.
Countries, by this standard, can subscribe to an international agreement, knowing full well that they can
interpret its clauses in a manner congruent with their
own beliefs.

Much of this repetitive discussion of UNESCO's
role in the free flow debate disregards the Third
World altogether. This is primarily because the free
flow concept is the stage of the power struggle between the East and the West. Second, the West is
threatened, for it stands to lose an important foothold in international relations and control of world
communications. The Soviet Union, alive to Third
World aspirations, poses as "a knight in shining ar-
mor" to reverse the tide of history, but also sees
the possibility of advancing its own clear international interests. By appearing as defender of the
Third World, it wishes to replace the West as the
leader of World Communications. And the Third World
looks to UNESCO to provide it with a certain tenuous
legality with which to make its presence felt.

154

Implications of the Declaration of the
Mass Media

For the Third World, UNESCO's Declaration of the Mass Media represented a triumph of sorts. The document is the first major declaration of principles, involving the uses of the mass media, setting standards and responsibilities for their operation. Also, it was a compromise between the seemingly more outrageous demands of the Nairobi conference, when the Soviet Union presented the controversial Draft, which threatened to destroy the conference, and the Western liberal position against any government interference in the mass media.

The Third World surrendered its insistence on Article XII of the original Nairobi Draft, which declared that "states are responsible for the activities in the international sphere of all mass media under their jurisdiction." For the West, it reaffirmed that UNESCO was to continue to be the place where international cooperation would be discussed. The Draft Declaration on the Mass Media was an acknowledgement by the West that it should look with less self-righteousness at its liberal tradition and be less critical of the Third World's attempts at solving complicated problems. In fact, these very attempts were recognized as well as the West's contribution to development.

The important gain for the Third World was a recognition that the Draft was a new beginning of an understanding of much that it had labored for at Nairobi, San Jose and the assorted meetings of the non-aligned countries group; namely, that their "aspirations, points of view and cultural identity be taken into due consideration" and that "a free flow and a wider and better balanced dissemination of information," was of critical importance to the continuing debate on the future of the international communications order.

Thus, UNESCO's Declaration of the Mass Media, without precisely stating so, agreed very much in spirit with the New International Information Order, which was indeed passed as a separate resolution at the 1978 General Conference, and later came to be adopted as part of the vocabulary of the non-aligned movement.

Third World gains are by no means complete or conclusive.

> Article I of the Declaration was concerned with the strengthening of peace and international understanding, the promotion of human rights and the countering of racialism, apartheid and incitement to war and a free flow and a wider and better balanced dissemination of information...This contribution will be the more effective to the extent that the information reflects the different aspects of the subject dealt with. 53/

Examples of the "different aspects" were not long in coming. At the 1979 Intergovernmental Conference on Communication Policies in Kuala Lumpur, Malaysia, the New Order was defined as "an integral part of efforts to achieve a new international economic order." As an influential writer elaborated:

> Imbalance and dependence are not left as undefined abstract notions but are specified in terms of colonialism and neo-colonialism... It is also significant that whereas the UNESCO Declaration begins by spelling out the freedom of information, the Kuala Lumpur declaration places freedom into a broader context of international relations and social responsibility. 54/

That the Kuala Lumpur conference went beyond and enlarged the Draft Declaration on the Mass Media is significant. It represented the concerns of the non-aligned countries, which had been in the vanguard of struggle for the Declaration and which saw the immediate parallel between the NIEO and the NIIO. By pushing the Western countries to the limits of their positions, they were able to abstract concessions in keeping with their own economic, political and social needs. Henceforth, much of the debate surrounding the NIIO and its relationship to the NIEO is conducted by the non-aligned movement, with temporary and sometimes capricious support from the socialist group countries.

The battle for the decolonization of world information channels continues. The main contention of the Third World, often repeated, is that the industrialized countries have developed their market

economies within a free flow of information system.
The main thrust of their attack is not at freedom of
information (although that is part of the problem,
too, and the argument here is on philosophical grounds
which attack the liberal position), but on the abuses
of it and the way how these affect the social and cultural milieu. That a majority of these countries have
sprung from the colonial tradition has but added fuel
to their complaints, for they are able to trace a long
relationship between the free market economies and the
freedom of information and the relationship of both to
social and cultural oppression. It is for this reason
that the NIIO and the NIEO are both very present mani-
festations of a past reality, smouldering beneath the
surface and seeking a future substantially different
from both the present and the past. The World Administrative Radio Conference provided the opportunity for
the revision of the radio spectrum. What really is at
stake, however, is the future distribution of international power.

Notes

1/ Condliffe, J. B. "Economic Power as an Instrument of National Policy." Papers and Proceedings of the 56th Annual Meeting of the American Economic Association, Washington, D. C., Jan. 1944, p. 307.

2/ Schiller, H. discusses this fully in Mass Communication and American Empire. New York: Augustus M. Kelley, 1969.

3/ Hazzard, S. Defeat of an Ideal. Boston: Little Brown, 1973, p. 84.

4/ Hazzard, S. Op. cit., "the U.S. from the outset has had proprietary feelings towards the United Nations not only as the Organization's chief sponsor but also because the founding principles, the "large pronouncements" of the United Nations are parallel and complementary to stated moral precepts of government in the U.S," p. 80.

5/ Rodney, W. How Europe Underdeveloped Africa. Washington, D.C. Howard University Press. This seminal work discusses the historical roots of this expansion.

6/ UNESCO, First Session of the General Conference, UNESCO, Paris, 1946.

7/ Report of the U.S. delegation with elected documents. U.S. Government Printing Office. Washington, D.C., 1947, p. 17.

8/ Yearbook on Human Rights for 1947. U.N. Lake success, N.Y., 1949, p. 439.

9/ Benton, W. Chairman, U.S. delegation to the Freedom of Information Conference, address delivered before the Anglo-American Press Club in Paris, April 7, 1948. Department of State Bulletin, April 18, 1948, pp. 518-519.

10/ Schiller, H. Op. cit., 1969.

11/ Tunstall, J. Op. cit., 1977.

12/ UNESCO. Report of the Montreal Conference. UNESCO, Paris, 1969.

13/ UNESCO, Op. cit., 1969.

14/ UNESCO, Op. cit., 1969.

15/ UNESCO. Report on Mass Media Channels in Latin America. UNESCO, Paris, 1961.

16/ UNESCO. Communications in Outer Space. UNESCO: Paris, 1967, p. 13.

17/ UNESCO. Television traffic-one-way street? Reports and Papers on Mass Communications. UNESCO. Paris, 1973.

18/ UNESCO. World Communications. UNESCO. Paris, 19

19/ UNESCO. Statistical Yearbook. UNESCO. Paris, 1970.

20/ UNESCO. Report to the United Nations Economic and Social Council on the Freedom of Information. UNESCO. Paris, 1975.

21/ International Press Institute. Report. Vienna, Austria, Dec. 1977, p. 3.

22/ Harms, L. S., J. Richstad, Kathleen A. Kie (ed.). Right to Communicate. Social Sciences and Linguistics Institute, University of Hawaii at Manoa, 1977, p. vii.

23/ UNESCO. Evaluation by the Director General of the Results of the First Development Decade in UNESCO's field of competence and Draft Program of the Organization for the Second Decade. UNESCO General Conference, Sixteenth Session, Paris, 1970 (16C/13).

24/ Naesselund, G. "Relations and perspectives within Development Support Communication, Communication Policy Research and Planning, and the Right to Communicate as seen by UNESCO." In Harms, Richstad, Kie (ed.), Right to Communicate. University of Hawaii, 1977.

25/ Naessulund. Op. cit., 1977.

26/ M'Bow quoted in Harms, Richstad and Kie, op. cit., 1977.

27/ d'Arcy, J. European Broadcast Union Review, 118 (1969), quoted in Harms, Richstad and Kie. Op. cit., 1977.

28/ Said, E. "Iran and the Press: Whose Holy War." Columbia Journalism Review. March-April 1980.

29/ UNESCO. Report of the Meeting of Experts on Communication Policies in Latin America. UNESCO. Paris, 1974.

30/ Communique of conference of non-aligned countries, Algeria, 1973.

31/ Op. cit., Non-Aligned Countries, 1973.

32/ Watts, A. Picture Tube Imperialism: The Impact of U.S. Television on Latin America. Maryknoll, N.Y.: Orbis Books.

33/ UNESCO. Report of the Meeting of Experts on Communication Policies in Latin America. UNESCO. Paris, 1974.

34/ Johnson, N. How to Talk Back to Your Television Set. Boston: Little Brown, 1970.

35/ Cole, Barry & Oettinger, M. Reluctant Regulators. Reading, Mass.: Addison Welsey Publishing Co., 1978.

36/ UNESCO. Op. cit., 1974.

37/ UNESCO. Report of the Meeting of Experts on Communication Policies in Latin America. UNESCO. Paris, 1974.

38/ UNESCO. Op. cit., 1974.

39/ The news agency business is encountering financial difficulty. UPI was put up for sale. The New York Times, October 1980.

40/ UNESCO. Op. cit., Quito, 1975.

41/ Ewen, S. Captains of Consciousness. New York: McGraw Hill, 1976.

42/ UNESCO. Report of the Meeting of Experts on Communication Policies in Latin America and the

Caribbean, San Jose, Costa Rica, 1976.

43/ Lent, J. "Caribbean Press Hemmed in with Controls." IPI Report, 25, 7 September 1976.

44/ Sussman, L. Mass Media and the Third World Challenge. Beverly Hills, Calif.: Sage Press, 1979.

45/ Crane, Rhonda J. The Politics of International Standards. Norwood, N.J.: Ablex Publishing Corporation, 1979.

46/ UNESCO. Report by the Director-General on the Intergovernmental Conference on Communication Policies in Latin America and the Caribbean. San Jose, 1976.

47/ The New York Times. April 7, 1980.

48/ The New York Times. Op. cit., 1980.

49/ Royal Commission on the Press. London: HMSO, 1977.

50/ Curran, J. "Press freedom as a property right: the crisis of press legitimacy," Media, Culture and Society. Vol. 1, No. 1. New York: Academic Press, 1979.

51/ Righter, R. Whose News. New York: Quadrangle, 1978.

52/ Nordenstreng, K. "Behind the Semantics - A Strategic Design," Journal of Communication. Vol. 29, No. 2, Spring 1979.

53/ UNESCO. Mass Media Declaration. UNESCO. Paris, 1978.

54/ Nordenstreng, K. Op. cit., 1979.

Chapter 6

PAST AND PRESENT CONSIDERED

Much of the recent history of information on the international scene has been influenced and promoted by those countries, which either by choice, conviction, or necessity, grouped themselves into a flexible alliance of non-alignment.

Their awakening came about as a result of several factors. First, was the development process, which revealed the significance of the old colonial channels of communication and their role in empire building and empire maintaining. Many of these countries were former colonies and had the opportunity to see the operation of these channels. And the close ties which existed and still do exist with metropolitan France has enabled Francophone countries to see at first hand the connection between information and control. Second, big power relations and the impossibility of playing any significant role alone, literally drove these countries together, despite obvious economic and political differences. Third, they realized that development was inseparable from knowledge and understanding of the communications process, whose channels were paradoxically introduced by industrialized countries, by means of development aid and other assorted aid schemes that involved an abundance of audio-visual equipment.

Non-alignment and information
at the crossroads

Tentative steps towards outlining and identifying areas of interest were taken at the Conference of Heads of State of Non-Aligned Countries at Algiers in 1973. Certain ideas in common currency were circulated with a view to facilitating greater exchanges. For example, they undertook to:

(1) reorganize existing communication channels which are the legacy of the colonial past and which have hampered free direct and fast communication between them,

(2) initiate action for the revision of existing multilateral agreements with a view to reviewing press cable rates and facilitating faster and cheaper intercommunication,

(3) take urgent steps to expedite the process of collective ownership of communication satellites and evolve a code of conduct for directing their use, and

(4) promote increased contact between the mass media, universities, libraries, planning and research bodies and other institutions so as to enable developing countries to exchange experience and expertise and share ideas. 1/

These early steps towards comprehensive information policy were later followed by several others that refined argument, and broadened areas of interest. For example, at the Non-Aligned Foreign Ministerial Conference at Lima in 1975, a resolution advocated cooperation in promoting information, reinforcing a significant effort in that field: the formation of the news agency pool by Tanjug, Yugoslavia. Also, advanced at Lima were ideas for sharing information; organization of forms of cooperation; mutual exchange of experiences in the information field, such as television and radio programs and, with an eye to the future, sought to prepare for the acquisition of satellites and a code to regulate the use of satellites.

Yugoslavia, one of the original countries of the non-aligned group, tried to bolster its influence and continue its leadership role by organizing seminars and colloquia for journalists. Information as a factor in cultural nationalism and as a crucial component for liberating nations from mental colonialism, was much discussed.

Meanwhile, the interests of the non-aligned group were echoed elsewhere. The Dag Hammarskjold Foundation sponsored in 1975 a study on world information as part of the problem of development. About the work of the Stockholm meeting, the Interim Report of the International Commission for the Study of Communication Problems said:

"Three trends may be said to have emerged from the discussions...on the present situation of information...the first trend is away from the rather simplistic approach of earlier years, which took account neither of the complexity nor the diversity of positions and towards a more sophisticated and in-depth, if somewhat tentative, analysis

164

of communication structures, operations
and content.

"The second trend reflects a more general
recognition of the existence of imbalance
in news flow, and, with reservations and
differences in interpretation, of distor-
tions in news presentations, the imbalance
being most noticeable in quantitative
terms - volume of information, but of
greater concern in qualitative terms -
content of information.

"The third trend is towards a general recognition of the importance of strengthening and diversifying news collection and
dissemination infrastructure in all countries, in stressing the complementary ways
in which national, regional, and transnational agencies develop and in proclaiming
the urgent need to extend and consolidate
international cooperation in this field."2/

The Stockholm meeting promoted a more than casual
interest in information dissemination patterns in the
world. One of these was the New York seminar held
later that very year, at which the relationship between information monopoly and economic power was the
object of more elaborate study. Among the recommendations were:

"1. that Third World countries as a whole,
at the regional and interregional levels,
should take steps to ensure that information and communication networks are used to
further and promote the establishment of
the New International Economic Order and
the objective of another development,

"2. to facilitate fundamental transforma-
tions to this end, governments should take
action within their countries to create,
foster and strengthen national structures,
based on self-reliance, for information and
communication that will enable them to
change existing systems in this field.

"3. national news agencies of Third World
countries should cooperate directly with

165

each other through bilateral arrangements
and through multilateral exchanges already
in existence or to be set up,

"4. early steps should be taken to set up
a Third World Information Centre to serve
Third World needs and to help in the dis-
semination of information on the Third
World in both industrialized and Third
World countries." 3/

Of these four recommendations, there is evidence
that 3 and 4 are well underway, and Third World news
agencies such as Tanjug and Inter Press Agency have
been pushing Third World independence from the established news agencies. The Latin American Institute
for Transnational Studies (ILET) is in the vanguard
of Third World establishments, monitoring information
flow among transnational corporations. Research on
alternative strategies for development is also part of
its work.

This sparse chronicle of the activities should not
distract from the significance of the conceptual aspects of the total movement. From its earlier preoccupation with international news flow and cultural content, it gravitated necessarily to political and economic considerations of dependency.

In fact, both in Tunis and Mexico City, a number
of papers dealt with the dependency aspect of international communications. For example, in Tunis, ILET
presented a paper on "the conceptual aspects for a
definition of the politics of news agencies;" and in
Algeria later that same year (1976), "the history of
news agency development and its effects in developing
countries," was considered. Other studies such as
"Mass Communications, the New International Economic
Order and Another Development," "A New World Communication and Information Structure" and "The Historical
Evolution of International News Agencies and their
Growth Towards Domination," indicated new directions.

A coherent set of objectives emerged in the non-
aligned movement, which might thus be summarized:

(1) To exert political pressure on behalf of
the developing world for liberation from the damaging
consequences of the present information system.

166

(2)   To assist in the creation of a new world information system, based less on a consumer-oriented
system, which reflect the values of the industrialized
countries that produce it.

(3)   To defend the rights of countries to full
sovereignty of the news and information process and to
the control of information within their borders.

(4)   To support the rights of access and participation of all sectors of the society in the news process.

(5)   To support and enlist the work of media in
national development and their role in the decolonization process.

These broad objectives were to be channelled into
work at the regional, national and international levels.
UNESCO, which increasingly came to acknowledge the objectives and the general thrust of the goals of the
non-aligned movement, included some of these in the
Draft Medium Term Plan, 1977/82.

Appraisal of information flow

The non-aligned countries were interested in
nothing less than a complete reappraisal of news values
and the concept of the world information system, which
had remained relatively unchanged since colonial times.
What these countries saw was a one-way flow of information and the institutionalizing of the news process by
a few news agencies. Their own efforts at news and information processing were slender compared to these
transatlantic giants and slowly the idea grew (there
was enough evidence to support it) that news agencies
should be subjected to a code of conduct and legislation to regulate their activities.

Coincident with these appraisals was the formulation of policy and guidelines for their own institutions. Typically, in those areas where government was
the sole and often the most affluent entrepreneur, it
should have more of a say in news and information dissemination. They were not unaware of the contradictions involved.

A free press and government are traditionally uncomfortable bedfellows. But there was also the other

side of the coin: if a press can operate freely, is it not contrary to the ideals of freedom to deny the government the same right. (It is sometimes conveniently forgotten that within a free press system, there is often significant pockets of government participation; and within the U.S. the International Communications Agency, which spawns the Voice of America, provide good copy; and Agence France Presse (AFP) has more than slender ties with the French Government. These contradictions remain so and any pretense that they can be resolved is idle. The need to bridge the gap between information affluence and information poverty is demanding.

The non-aligned countries also were well aware that however searching reappraisals were, they could not be a substitute for complete overhaul of a system in which their own participation had been minimal. Their present needs required a greater share in the total development of international preferential rate-structures and satellites. They believe that inroads into the international communications system should also be accompanied by promotion and development of alternatives to the existing international structure. These are no easy objectives; indeed, the first task was recognition of their importance.

The industrial world, which had traditionally exploited them, had to become aware that what is involved is no less than the future of the world. They could not separate themselves from that which they had once dominated. Splendid isolation was an outmoded doctrine, which provided little comfort. To promote this understanding required education; and the vast and pervasive resources of the mass media would seek to inform, explain, and enlarge upon the collective consciousness about the needs of development and particularly that of alternative information networks.

This mammoth undertaking was to be at the multilateral, regional and international levels. It was to involve general questions, relating to the transfer of technology, identification of common interests and possible tangents of cooperation between the industrialized and the non-industrialized world, and an expansion of the relations between countries to the North and those to the South, euphemistically referred to as the North-South dialogue. (The author prefers the more general world "relations", as dialogue is for equals

168

and this has been sorely lacking among these groups of
countries: and patronage, the more familiar level of
discourse is not the same as dialogue.)

More specifically, the non-aligned movement wished
to study the free flow of information, and questions
allied to it, such as governmental participation as
well as private commercial interests, new information
flow models, and the feasibility of institutions which
would foster development and training.

Development and related problems hinged on adequate communications efficiently administered and supported by joint cooperative measures, in which their
countries would take part.

There was need for this, for financial and other
considerations. Cooperative measures assumed the
sharing of facilities and experts in short supply. They
entailed the development of exchanges at bilateral and
multilateral levels and following this, a study into
the possibilities of acquiring satellites. These plans
required an organizational structure, which could be
a clearinghouse for information and plans, a focus of
energies that would operate on several different levels
simultaneously. For example, they would provide opportunities and facilities for the exchange of audio-
visual programs, encourage professional relations among
member countries by organizing conventions and meetings
and seminars. Achieved would be more than a non-
aligned center of information, but a repository of the
new concept of information and culture. It would stimulate scholarly exchanges through scholarships and
fulfil the objective of international public relations
and national education.

These ambitious forays in the international world
would be matched with equally spirited attempts on
each separate national scene. Indeed, national communication policies, emphasizing comprehensive planning
and development, would become the vehicle for disseminating information about the New International Information Order (NIIO); and national news agencies would
seek to ensure that news was related to the social,
cultural and economic needs of the people. Thus, the
relation of national news agencies to the New International Information Order would be complete. The
former was a part of that total movement of non-aligned
countries, the so-called poor South, which in the interests of greater cooperation and leverage, allied

themselves to a new concept, whose central objective
was to revise the balance of forces which "ruled" the
world. In this respect the NIIO was directly related
to the New International Economic Order (NIEO), whose
governing philosophy is no less than the total revision of economic relations among countries.

Information and internationalism

The imperatives of an industrial culture promoted
the development and growth of international information
structures. Countries that have an interest in empire
have an abiding stake in controlling the information
processes. The American Revolution dates the modern
information process upon which the free market economy depends. 4/ The colonial powers relied on information to serve an economic system, in which power centralized, radiated to the periphery. Control was
therefore an easy task and propaganda a means of its
exercise. Both national and international structures
were dominated by control of information by the ruling
class, variously referred to as aristocracy, bourgeoisie,
industrial magnates, international cartels, transnational corporations and industrial magnates.

Information and its fellow traveller economic
exploitation were responsible, therefore, for the close
alliances between colonial power and colony. It is
interesting to speculate on the relative importance of
the control exercised by various colonial powers. In
the case of France, the cultural component succeeded
in welding together a more cohesive and longer-lasting
empire than the case of England. With the latter the
absence of a significant cultural relations made the
colonial ambitions somewhat tenuous and less close
knit. The consequence of this can be seen to this day,
where a former French colony still enjoys (?), despite
a residue of colonial hostility, a cultural relationship with France that a former English colony has to
strive for. A further consequence is that the lack of
a cultural point of reference enables the latter to
more quickly develop local institutions.

The colonial relationship is the key to understanding the continuing traffic of information and internationalism. In fact, on gaining independence, many of
the former colonies adopted the informational structures of the bygone era. Many also were encouraged to
do so, for the continued existence of these structures
ensured that the lines of communication remained in

existence and that the common information exploitation
axis continued. How else is the installation of sophisticated television resources in parts of Francophone Africa to be explained, when clearly the indigenous needs are quite different. (The Ivory Coast is
one such, Gabon is another and Zaire is the most extravagant case.)

The structure of dependency thus was maintained
and indeed encouraged by both parties to the depend-
ency-colonial power and former colony--and in place
of the overt information-propaganda-control syndrome,
came more alluring and interesting entertainment programs, less overtly propagandistic but equally as
dangerous. Thus control, surrendered at independence,
still came to be exercised as a result of the information process, which still is controlled by the colonial powers, now part of the transnational corporations.
Their interests protected by local and frequently national legislation and defense alliances, have been
free to prescribe, and carve territory relatively un-
encumbered by ideological and other considerations.
France's involvement in the civil war in the Republic
of Chad provides good copy.

It is ironic that the very economic expansion informed the Third World of the importance of information
on the national and international agenda. The economic imbalance of world trade, which was a prelude to
the deliberations for the NIEO, focused attention on
the role of information. Information was identified
as a component of colonization and demands for its
decolonization called for. Colonization was acknowledged not as a purely political process, in which
attitudes of mind were crucial, but as a philosophy
or way of being, incorporating all aspects of existence.

Given the firm connection between information and
communication and the colonial process, the emancipa-
tion of information from its colonial associations had
certain implications at both national and international levels. At the national, it meant media freedom
and the opportunity for individuals and groups to participate in the public agenda. Internationally, it
aimed at the "democratization of international information networks," an end to the domination of transnational corporations, which controlled worldwide communications, and the beginning of alternative considerations.

One of the alternatives considered was communications as a total process. Communication policies and planning would, under this new dimension, be less an exclusive affair of politicians and elites. The point of view was expressed that the mass media should be more broadly representative; and there is every good reason why this should be. For one thing, national development depends on wide support which can be promoted and enhanced through the communications process. In fact, a multitude of studies show the significance of information diffusion for development. 5/

Communications planning is indispensable to the overall development process. Lack of development is not simply an economic factor, but an information one as well. For what the Third World needs and asks for is the power to define itself within its own cultural frame of reference and not within the framework of the advanced industrial societies. For an objective of such magnitude, it needs efficient national planning based on priorities.

Efficient planning and national priorities raises the question of the means to attain this end. The ability to process information is the key, and the Third World suffers in two respects: a surfeit of information in some few cases, and a scarcity of information in others. Also, the information available has been identified with social, cultural and national life of industrialized countries. Information has never been considered a national resource reflecting social and cultural and political realities, in which freedom of the individual to seek as well as to impart information is a fundamental part of social organization.

Technology provides the means to harness knowledge and to share information, but there has not been a systematic attempt to see information as part of the total needs of a society, and an integral part of its functioning. Transnational corporations, which function for profit, see only that which supports their aims and use whatever means for the continuance of those aims. News agencies are often not capable of grasping the importance of news for particular national interests and what they sell reflects attitudes often at odds with the values of particular societies. In addition, the mass media, which depend on the news agencies, work according to the demands of the marketplace. They are prisoners of their own structure, and confined within narrow limits of profit and influence, which, "although fascinating...unfortunately is of little help in assessing the implications or high stakes of recent technological developments." 6/

"Information is a basic resource...that is central to the conduct of international relations." Anthony Oettinger, Director of the Harvard Program on Technology and Society, suggests that information is a unifying concept, which should be subject to government policy.7/ This is to take a systems view of information and communications. It is to see them both as necessary for the functioning of modern society, at the national and international levels. At the former level, information should be focused at the "inclusion of every individual in the processes of communication that shape societies." 8/ Internationally, it should move towards "the democratization of international information networks, at the establishment of horizontal instead of vertical structures, and at the conceptualization of "alternative" information sources. 9/

As far as the Third World is concerned, these new ideas are not academic, but relate to vital interests. The unifying concept of information mentioned relates to certain very real questions such as "what information is flowing, for whose benefit, to whose detriment, and at what costs or risks."

The U.S. government placed these questions within the context of national security interests in three days of Congressional hearings on the New International Information Order. Questions which indicated vital national interests were:

How can the flow of information be increased
to better all mankind without impinging upon
personal privacy, proprietary data and national security?

How can, or should, the Second and Third
World's desire to rigidly control information sectors of their societies be accommodated, while trying to allow free flow
of information worldwide?

How can the U.S. Government organize to protect our security, cultural and economic
interests and also help meet the needs, and

173

gain the cooperation, of the developing
nations? 10/

Study of communication problems speaks pointedly
to the issue:

> The concept of free flow of information as
> it has been invoked for the past thirty
> or so years, and as it is applied today,
> can serve to justify a doctrine serving
> the interests of the powerful countries
> or groups which all too frequently ena-
> bles them to ensure or to perpetuate
> cultural domination under the cloak of
> generous ideas. 11/

The concept of freedom of information is the bul-
wark of U.S. democracy and the pillar of freedom of
speech, civil liberties and the free market economy.
The NIIO appears to threaten these foundations.

A clue to the thinking of the Third World was
provided at the Nairobi General Conference of UNESCO,
when the U.S. offered $25 million for research into
the use of satellites for development process. While
this is a worthwhile endeavor (and at the same time
a compromise, allowing for agreement), it does not
solve the problem of balanced communication between the
Third World and the industrialized countries, the
North and the South. In fact, it can make matters
worse, for it can perpetuate a dependency from which
the Third World is trying to escape. The export of
sophisticated technology will have to be failored to
local needs and resources in order to be effective.

But the export of valuable technology has certain
obvious dangers. As long as the industrialized countries are in the ascendancy, exports do not pose a
problem. But what of the future? There is no guarantee that this will remain unchallenged. The same
countries which today support the doctrine of the free
flow of information might find themselves at a later
date opting for a balanced flow because interests are
jeopardized. Canada now limited the entry of foreign-
made entertainment programs, raising the specter of
trade protectionism. Countries reserve the right to
decide where their best interests are and Canada, by
no means a Third World country, addressed one of the
concerns of the NIIO; namely, that information structures be in tune with the social, economic and

cultural interests of societies which support them; and this is not to say that they should unilaterally pursue interests at the expense of the international community. The whole point of the NIIO is that "information in the modern world is characterized by basic imbalances, reflecting the general imbalance that affects the international community." 12/ The significance of which is detailed consideration of what these imbalances are, in what ways they manifest themselves, their importance in the North-South dialogue, their political and economic, social and cultural ramifications, remedies for them and the conceptualization of a new order.

The New International Information Order considered

Imbalances in the international communications system grew with concern for poverty and underdevelopment. The two coincided with the Third World's realization that information was part of the process of decolonization necessary for economic, political and cultural independence. Information imbalance was just one of the less obvious forms that divided the world. The relations between the technologically rich and control of the world's channels of information were not accidental. The power of the few exists in a legion of ways, but especially in the political, legal and technico-financial spheres.

Mustapha Masmoudi, a former Secretary of State for Information in Tunisia, the author of the statement of the NIIO, points to the many forms these imbalances take in the political arena: a flagrant quantitative imbalance between North and South; an inequality in information resources; a de facto hegemony and a will to dominate; a lack of information on developing countries; survival of the colonial era; an alienating influence in the economic, social and cultural spheres. 13/

These represent a catalogue of grievances against the industrialized countries. The five news agencies which together control and monopolize news systems, perpetuate a system of dependency within the Third World. Inequality in the radio spectrum which is controlled by a few countries (until the World Administrative Radio Conference, 1979, the U.S. controlled 90 percent of the radio spectrum) also exists.

The influence of the mass media and the will to
dominate, continues Masmoudi, derives from "financial,
industrial, cultural and technological interests and
are exercised by means of control of information in
which transnational enterprises play a dominant part.
The power to control accompanies the power to determine the public agenda of the Third World. Also, it
is the will to affect the cultural values of three-
quarters of the world. Thus, the transnational corporations have an interest in maintaining the status
quo through cultural imperialism which includes advertising, magazines and television programs. 14/ To
control the messages of a culture is to influence the
manner in which it celebrates itself: to define it.
Paralysis in the fact of transnational control is
complete. Through the harvest of television programs,
books, magazines, films, which daily find their way
to the Third World, cultural supremacy of the industrialized countries is guaranteed and the consumer,
avid for more of the same gloss, becomes an eager
participant in the economic exchange of his country's
own limited foreign currency. It is not without some
reason that the control of the mass media in some of
these countries, is in the hands of the upper middle
class, which sector defends the status quo, in order
to ensure its privileges. Thus, the transnational
corporations have their own staunch local defenders.
And the majority of the people, alienated from their
culture, becomes culturally deprived, passive recipients rather than active participants in a cultural
experience. The crisis is therefore one of psychic
proportions, in which an estranged psyche cannot
fully contribute to the national development process.
The free flow of information ensures that this practice continues.

The free flow of information stems from the
liberal philosophy, which has been at the heart of
Western academy. Thus, the expansion of trade, com-
merce and culture, which is a part of commerce, is
defended within the legal framework of these countries. The NIIO addresses issues which international
law treats with scant respect and little attention:
individual rights and community rights; freedom of
information or freedom to inform; right of access to
information sources; the ineffectiveness of the right
to correction; the absence of an international deon-
tology and the defective character of the regulations
governing the profession; imbalance in the field of
copyright; imbalance in the distribution of the

source of the spectrum; disorder and lack of coordination in telecommunications and in the use of satellites,
compounded with flagrant inequalities between states
in this field. 15/

The free flow doctrine "defends" the rights of the
communicator, the institution, the transnational, but
the responsibilities of the receiver of the message,
the public, the citizen are not mentioned. This omission allows for the one-way flow of information, which
gives power to the communicator at the expense of the
receiver. International copyright is an example, whose
"protectionist effects...while at the same time fostering the circulation of intellectual works from the industrialized countries to developing countries, it has
benefitted the latter not at all." 16/ The same might
be said of the radio spectrum whose unequal distribution sanctioned by the World Administrative Radio Conference of 1959, allowed the industrialized countries
to obtain a lion's share of it. 17/ The on-going battle to revise the legal structure of international communications is focused on four areas, where low tariffs
have helped in the establishment and maintenance of
technological supremacy and the perpetuation of a monopoly telecommunications; satellites; distribution of
radio frequencies; transport of publications.

But international negotiation is a slow process,
especially now when the time for change is recognized.
The objectives of the NIIO are to bring about change
in the Third World's perception of itself and the industrialized world's understanding that the basis upon
which its supremacy has rested, cannot continue, for it
will eventually bring about a crisis from which no
party will gain, or emerge unscathed.

For the Third World, the objectives must be to
increase and broaden the possibilities for access
and participation by individuals, citizens, groups,
and governments; to institutionalize national media
and ensure that information circulates the society
and supports national development policies; to train
personnel to encourage international exchanges and
cooperation among the non-aligned countries and developed countries and the international organizations.

For industrialized countries, the objectives are
clear. They are called upon to educate their people
about world interdependence; to "balance" the information flow, assume a more sensitive position with

177

regard to the culture of countries dissimilar to theirs and to pay more attention to the news and news agencies of Third World countries.

For international organizations, the objectives are equally demanding. They must assist in the welfare of the Third World media development by granting technical and financial assistance for research and development schemes and historical documentation; and "devise a clear-cut policy on the use of satellite transmission systems, representing in all cases the sovereign rights of individual states." 18/

Curriculum for world order

The NIIO is part of a global concept for the equitable distribution of information and other resources and related to the NIEO, which exercised the Club of Rome. The authors explain that "this economic dependence (the Third World's) is rooted in the main institutions of the international system created largely by the industrialized countries to deal essentially with their own problems at a time in which the voices of the world's poor was unheard in international fora." 19/ And Sir Arthur Lewis explains that this international system is based not on the just principle of equal pay for equal work, 20/ and because of which, "the Third World is insisting on fundamental structural change." 21/

Information and its dissemination is a means of enhancing the growth of the Third World, which requires new strategies and a commitment to institutional change by the industrialized countries.

Information is not now treated as a necessary tool for living, but is "one of the fundamental human rights--individual as well as collective--since it is an essential component in the improvement of mankind and in the capacity for development of societies." 22/ Access and participation are necessary ingredients of this process. But "until such time as information and communication patterns are liberated from the market-oriented sensationalism and news presentation," 23/ development will remain incomplete. The liberation of minds from the demands of the marketplace, can only take place with education and the role of the mass media as an education tool is especially important for a curriculum of world information and education.

This curriculum must address the issues of the continuity of life on earth, the responsibility for power, means for the preservation of life; investigate and research a whole range of policy issues, living standards, the quality of life, given reduced expectations; and the nature of international relationships in a changing era.

The governments of industrialized countries will share with their citizens the news that there is an inequitable distribution of power in the world; that there is need to change this; that technology provides the means to free the world from the shackles of oppression, conformity and injustice. Such a curriculum, harnessed to the pervasive resources of the mass media, can succeed in winnowing public opinion from lethargy and ignorance of the burning issues of the day, and prepare it for the adoption of structural changes in international relationships.

The curriculum for world order is based on a perception of the world as interdependent and composed of a harmony of parts, even if not a harmony of ideas and people. The mission must be a knowledgeable citizen, alive to responsibilities both to country and to the world. Such a citizen must realize that his survival is not unilateral, but multilateral in the sense that it is bound to the citizen of another country.

The study of information in this curriculum will include the capacity and ability to use technology to increase the flow of information around the world and to ensure that channels of information are at the disposal of many more people than they presently are. This will result in greater communication between leaders and people, for the multiple channels would encourage two-way communication. In such a climate public opinion becomes less the exertions of a privileged elite than the reflections of national conscience. Leaders cannot then claim that they had nothing to guide them. Multiple channels of communication would stimulate an awareness of international affairs. As various national groups coalesce, there would be a tendency for similar groups elsewhere to do likewise and with that, the likelihood of influence and pressure brought to bear on governments and international fora. This would facilitate the adjustment procedures so necessary for any fundamental change between the industrialized countries and the Third

179

World and the transnational concerns that are part of
the former.

Global strategy for a more equitable distribution
of resources is not intended as an exercise confined
to the elite of various societies, who in the process
of time would come to understand its wider implications.
It would be a pointless exercise if change embraces
only the chosen few who are aware of its importance.
It is not a temporary expedient to aid a troubled
world out of a difficult situation, with the understanding that the status quo would resume at a favorable
opportunity. It is a need for a more understanding and
productive world as it confronts the issues of survival.
Clearly then, the curriculum for survival must be one
that is comprehensive, and include the education of all
citizens.

The scope of the curriculum must be an integral
part of secondary schools, universities, continuing
and adult education. Already there is some evidence
of this with the spread of interdisciplinary courses,
and area studies at the larger universities in the
field is Syracuse University's Maxwell School of Citi-
zenship and Public Affairs, the Newhouse School of
Communications and the Department of Instructional
Technology of the same university. And at governmental
level, the International Communications Agency and
others continue their labors.

Curriculum must not only consider political, economic and cultural issues as factors that contribute
to survival; it must also address specific questions,
such as the right to respond by Third World countries,
which find themselves the objects of bias and discrimination; the security of news reporters within Third
World countries, a question tied to the role of transnational news corporations; and finally, the nature
and ideology of technical cooperation.

The Third World too must apply itself to this
curriculum. These countries must work towards incorporating greater access and participation by their
citizens in the communications process, even as they
strive to increase channels of communication and work
internationally towards a new understanding with the
industrialized world.

The objectives of the non-aligned movement are
part of this curriculum and include: the right of

180

self-determination of all colonial peoples; the need to
preserve world peace and especially to prevent a nuclear
confrontation between the U.S. and the Soviet Union; to
eradicate racism in all its forms; to restructure the
old economic order and to reduce the disparity between
the poor and the rich nations in the world; and to improve communication among all peoples and to restructure the existing communication system that has tended
to be monopolistic and against the aspirations of the
dispossessed nations. 24/

These objectives have both an external as well as
an internal validity. Internally, a system of national
priorities has to be set up and planning with a viable
communications component instituted. Externally, well-
defined policies of economic cooperation and technical
assistance, approved by themselves and under the umbrella, if necessary, of a United Nations agency,
should prove beneficial. Moreover, they should strive
to enhance national culture, protecting it from the
more violent incursions of the media of industrialized
countries. At the same time, these objectives should
define a permanent place for information and culture
within national planning. The organization of information and culture to fit the specific needs of individual countries encourages self-reliance and strength.
Thus, alternative forms of communication can be ex-
plored within the context of national communications
planning and less emphasis placed on electronic media.

Third World initiative

An initiative designed to make a dent in the information imbalance was the creation of the Non-Aligned
Press Pool, which came into operation following the
the Fourth Non-Aligned Summit in Algiers in 1973.

Tanjug, the headquarters of the Pool and the national press agency of Yugoslavia, expanded its international operations by signing agreements with 75 news
agencies, including the big five, Associated Press,
United Press International, Reuters, Agence France
Presse and Tass. The agreements between Tanjug and the
foreign news agencies generally established cooperation in four major fields: exchange of news, assistance to permanent correspondents, projects requiring
special assistance and technical cooperation. 25/
Tanjug, supported by Samarchar, India's news agency,
concentrates on news coverage not likely to be picked
up by the other agencies, or news which is "cooperative

rather than conflict-oriented." 26/

Predictably, Western news agencies saw sinister
possibilities for government propaganda emanating from
Tanjug and flooding the Third World. But the news
agency has gone about its business with hardly a stir
on the international scene. In fact, a study indicated that there is some sharing of news with the big
five as well as with others; 27/ and the strident
voices proclaiming the certain defeat of free market
economies by the spread of evil Marxist doctrines, is
largely baseless. 28/

Yet, despite this implied criticism, the Pool does
not pretend to be a news agency. It is what its name
implies, a clearinghouse of information from whatever
source it comes, with the bulk of the distribution done
by Tanjug and regional centers in Tunisia and Cuba. It
has been suggested that the objectives of Tanjug, which
are cooperation between mutual partners "on the basis
of mutual respect" is at odds with government controlled
news agencies.

The objections and criticism of Third World attempts at a novel and admittedly, in the view of the
author, far from perfect institutions are those which
concern values. The Western view is that news must be
objective and free from any taint whatever. The Third
World's view is that news cannot be objective and there
is little point arguing about it. 29/ Since this is
the case, then let the reader be the judge. If, as
one critic points out, government news "will bore
readers abroad as much as the same items bore readers
at home," 30/ the same is equally true of news from
Reuters, Associated Press and others, which relates
to national disasters, catastrophes; people in the
Third World might be more interested in questions which
lie closer to them. One writer claims that crisis
themes such as unrest and dissent, war, terrorism,
crime, coups and assassinations and disasters received
more coverage than non-crises, such as political-
military, economics, environment, technology--science
and human interest. 31/ This is only partly due to
"television's attraction to visually exciting material." More ie explained by the audience's conditioning
which is fostered by the international media. A South
American scholar assesses the incidence of this in that
continent. 32/

Additional criticism of the Third World news agency pool is that views will be a convenient substitute for news and the audience will suffer because of this. Judgements of value are inseparable from news and it is self-righteous to expect that it should not accompany Third World news agency efforts; at least, hopefully, the values would be such as are congruent with their own policies.

But as unannounced, unspoken fear is that the international news enterprises are about to lose their monopoly in a highly profitable part of the world. (While it might not be profitable in financial terms, it is profitable in prestige and the news agencies need the international exposure in order to stimulate the home market, especially at a time when demand for news is increasing.) The diffusion of television receivers in South Korea has been spectacular; 33/ and in Venezuela, the annual growth rate of television sets is 11 percent, with 92 percent of the households in Caracas having one television set and 48 percent of the rural areas. 34/ Thus, the expansion of television receivers takes in both town and country.

The expansion is not limited to television. Researchers found that for one week, Third World newspapers were ahead of those in the U.S. and the Soviet Union in the amount of space devoted to international news. 35/ Third World audiences are discovering that news and information are inseparable from the important tasks of development and the responsibilities of nation-building. This trend appears to be happening at all levels of society. 36/ Irrespective of political and other factors, the audience is acquiring a sophistication of its own and participating in its own decolonization, freeing itself from traditional patterns of behavior, throwing off the shackles of the past and forging ahead to redefine a reality of its own. Examples of this abound and the World Administrative Radio Conference provides good copy.

World Administrative Radio Conference

The issues that the WARC was called upon to face from September 24 to December 6, 1979 were complex. The purpose of the conference was to revise the radio spectrum in the light of changing and changed telecommunication needs at a time when "the use of the radio spectrum has gradually opened up a new and extremely complex set of political questions concerning how this resource is to be shared among different societies, between governments and citizens, and between different kinds of service." 37/

There had been significant changes since the last conference in 1959; new nations had come into being, demanding additional services. Communications technology had become increasingly advanced and those countries that could afford it were leaving the others behind. International law was sought to sanction their expansion and growing consumption of the available radio spectrum.

But also significant were factors, which had not yet divided the world and about which a number of observers had written. First, the current membership of the International Telecommunications Union (ITU) was divided between Third World countries and the industrialized, exacerbated perhaps by the now familiar North-South division. Second, was the all too usual division between the rich countries and the poor countries, the rich having the technological capability to dispose of the spectrum in a manner that they pleased and those countries that did not have the resources to do so.

These factors determined the negotiating positions. The Third World countries wanted assurance that places on the spectrum would be guaranteed them, when they had the necessary technology. They supported the so-called a priori position. Industrialized countries, led by the U.S., which had 90 percent of the spectrum, wished to retain their prerogatives on the basis of first come, first served.

The stakes were high, for increased communications traffic demanded more frequency space and the higher the frequency, the more possibilities for information transmission. Thus, the continuing exercise for new ways of expanding the available spectrum continually occupies technical experts. But one cannot separate technical niceties from political and international affairs, especially since technological know-how is a factor in political power. And the Third World did not wish to pawn its chances for the future because of a present lack of technology, or be pushed aside to the higher reaches of the spectrum which, though less congested, are more expensive to operate from.

184

Industrialized countries divided along those general lines; the U.S. in particular, was extraordinarily concerned with the space availability for satellites and Third World access to the radio spectrum. It was easy to see why. Priori planning to guarantee shortwave frequencies for future use by Third World countries, would be at the expense of its military communications system. Also, prior planning would hinder satellite development for peaceful purposes.

The Third World countered that prior planning would encourage not hinder development of satellites and be an effective beacon for the future. This view is in keeping with the U.S. domestic situation, where the Federal Communications Commission (FCC) has consistently allocated channels for use by public radio against the incursions from the commercial markets.

The resolution of the conference seemed to favor the a priori approach of the Third World, though not decisively so. A future conference slated for 1984 would resolve space and frequency allocations. Significant though was the voting strength of the Third World, which was able to wield a united front for what were perceived as just demands. But the shape of the future is likely to be one of compromise, where the industrialized countries, given time to realize a more coherent plan to satisfy the Third World, would in fact seize the opportunity during the five-year interim.

Wider international contact

The limited accomplishments of the IRAC were an impetus for the movement to broaden international communications. And at the next UNESCO-sponsored Intergovernmental Conference on Communication Policies in Africa in July 1980, in the Cameroun Republic, the Yaounde Declaration underlined African solidarity "to work with all our strength for changes called for by the present world situation, so that every people may freely inform and be informed, full respect being accorded to their dignity." 38/

The recommendations of the conference ranged over a wide area: communication policies; language policies; traditional modes of communication; technological issues; broadcasting; storage of information; information flow; communication satellites; research and training; African regional cooperation and unity; international cooperation. These were an acknowledgement

185

of the complexities of development, which face the whole continent; moreover, one in which "few countries... now possess adequate means of apprehending the facts of their own situation, and at the regional level it is rare for information to circulate directly from country to country." 39/ Above all, the recommendations helped clarify by defining the limits of their ambitions.

But the Yaounde Declaration was important for other reasons. First, it represented a charter for the present and future of national development, in which communication and culture are assigned prominent roles.

Second, it underscored that relations between Africa and the rest of the world would be based on equal partnership. African countries, alive to the possibility that so much of their present needs are part of the thrust for change in the international system and therefore seen as a threat, held out the olive branch, inviting cooperation rather than conflict. True, this was done before (the history of the non-aligned movement is taken up with the desire for change of one kind or another); but, it was the first time that such a conference canvassed opinion so widely and openly about how to bring it about in the information sphere.

Third, the conference made specific reference to the importance of interpersonal communication and the traditional African forms of communication, which rely on dialogue. Aware of the swift advance of modern communications technology, it stressed the symbiotic relationship between the old and the new, the traditional and modern. In fact, the burning question of communications technology in the Third World is the extent to which technology and institutional processes share the lives of the citizen, gives it meaning, depth and dignity. But technology for education, culture and nation-building needs skills and resources which are in short supply; and the International Program for the Development of Communication (IPDC), recommended by the Intergovernmental Conference for Cooperation on Activities, Needs and Programmes relating to the Development of Communications in Paris, April 1980, was suggested as an appropriate funding agency. 40/

To a great and, perhaps, reassuring degree, these recommendations, except for that which dealt with information flow--the cause of so much of past and future concerns--contained no surprises. African countries saw the Declaration on the Mass Media as paving the way for the removal of global barriers to communication.

The conference also stressed the need for training skilled personnel and recommended that journalists be assured of protection in the carrying out of their duties. It was this clause that caused a great flurry among Western countries, when the New World Information Order came to be debated at the 21st General Conference in Yugoslavia, September 1980.

UNESCO's twenty-first General Conference at Yugoslavia

This Conference took place against a background of the Report of the International Commission for the Study of Communication Problems, which had been set up after the stormy Nairobi meeting, when the debate centered on the still controversial Draft Declaration on the Mass Media. Following Nairobi, the Commission met under the chairmanship of Sean McBride, the former Irish Foreign Minister and Nobel Peace Prize winner. Given the heated discussions of the day, it was clear that the Commission would have a range of prickly questions to study though not to resolve. The job "of studying the totality of the problems of communication in the contemporary world" was indicative of the enormity of what it set out to do.

The Commission saw "three questions at the heart of the international debate."

The first relates to the dimensions of the liberation and independence of peoples, and may affect the ever precarious process of building and safeguarding peace...

The second question relates to the conceptual foundations of development. The conception of development as a linear, quantitative and exponential process, based on transfers of imported and frequently alienating technology, is beginning to be replaced by the vision of an endogenous, qualitative process focused on man and his vital needs, aimed at eradicating inequalities and based on appropriate technologies which respect the cultural context

187

and generate and foster the active participation of the populations concerned. 41/

But there were other questions, no less sensitive,
no less vital to the understanding of the age; communication: its structures and actors; socio-economic,
socio-political and socio-cultural effects; problems
today; trends, prospects and ambitions.

The tone of the final Report showed an awareness
of the immensity of the problems facing countries.
Descriptive and analytic in lay-out, it documented, explained, suggested, recommended, paving the way--it
must have believed--for constructive consideration and
eventual action.

Certain clauses bear examination: it condemned
censorship unequivocally, but included a Soviet dissent that viewed censorship as a national rather than
an international one. It defended the right of journalists to free access to resources; but also included a
Third World objection to "colonialist domination" of
news distribution. Access to resources, which was an
important consideration by Western countries, was defended as "an indispensable requirement for accurate
and balanced reporting." Recognizing that "the full
and factual presentation of news about one country to
others is a continuing problem," it insisted that access "involves unofficial, as well as official sources
of information." With regard to inaccurate or mali-
cious reporting, the Commission preferred to leave it
to the individual countries to determine how correct-
ions and replies should be applied.

The McBride Report also dealt with a number of
delicate issues: one such was the threat to journalists
and a code of ethics. An earlier position supported
the idea that journalists should be protected in their
work from the hazards of the marketplace; but this was
dropped because of the possibility that it could lead
to government licensing of journalists. But the code
of ethics and the "right to reply to inaccurate reports" was a prominent part of the study. Indeed, the
Report maintained: "the concept of freedom with responsibility necessarily includes a concern for professional ethics...The adoption of codes of ethics at national and, in some cases regional level, is desirable,
provided that such codes are prepared and adopted by
the profession itself--without governmental interference. 42/

Thus, the concerns of the Western countries, which saw the freedom of journalists impaired by unfortunate influences, were in large measure unfounded. The McBride Report indicated that such changes that could be brought about in the international practice of journalism, should not be at the expense of freedom in the traditional sense and meaning of the term; but if the journalist was to be free, then he should exercise that freedom in a responsible way and not commit espionate under cover of professionalism, a practice which it condemned.

The Report persuaded both the Third World and the industrialized countries of the importance of cooperation and mutual assistance. It sought to extend the concept of communication freedom from an individual right to a collective right, advocating "all those working in the mass media (to)...contribute to the fulfillment of human rights, both individual and collective, in the spirit of the UNESCO Declaration on the Mass Media, the Helsinki Final Act, and the International Bill of Human Rights." 43/ Censorship of any kind could play no part in international conduct.

Attention was paid the activities of the transnational corporations and "effective legal measures should be designed to limit the process of concentration and monopolization." 44/ The thrust of the main body of the Report was to widen public participation in the decision-making process through structures that would promote this and by such access as would encourage the open interchange of ideas.

Clear as this challenge to the world community to set up structures to enhance public and community participation, it was more its international significance that the McBride Commission was concerned with. Such "economic discrepancies" as existed everywhere should no longer be countenanced and "the very notion of a new world information and communication order presupposes fostering international cooperation" which includes international assistance and contributions towards international understanding.

The Report intended its recommendations to serve as a background statement for the new international information, and communication order (NIIO); and to that extent it succeeded. It delineated areas of special and specific concern to the international

189

community, to the Third World and the developed countries and designated areas, which merit further study.

But its reception in Yugoslavia was far from acceptable by Western powers in general, and all their
collective fears about news management were violated.
They abhorred what it implied and detested some of its
ambiguous phraseology. "We reject the notion that the
news media should be coerced into serving as a tool for
social and economic policy." 45/ Still, the West
agreed to the provisions of the NIIO, even though support for the Palestine Liberation Organization's propaganda effort, and a code of journalistic ethics,
seemed a far cry from its own traditions. 46/

Their refusal to fully accept the Third World's
position is understandable and regardless of the pronouncements of UNESCO, they will not allow that organization to define their information policy. And the
Soviet Union, which has tried and continues to do so,
to get UNESCO to endorse its dictatic governmental
policy, will not rest its case.

The Third World's position has centered on control of information channels and resources, and on the
desire for more power and influence within the United
Nations and other international associations. They
have used the information issue to assault the Western
Achilles heel, hoping thereby to extract concessions
on other fronts; and the NIIO is but part of a wider
canvas for power in all international bodies, by re-
vising the rules of the game--the World Bank, the International Monetary Fund, the World Administrative
Radio Conference, the General Agreement on Tariffs and
Trade and the International Telecommunications Union
and the Conference on the Law of the Sea--are prime
targets. This explains the feverish campaign for a New
International Economic Order and the vigor with which
it is pursued.

But at the level of practical possibilities, the
Third World's position is realizable only in a limited
way. Perhaps this is why the debate is so finesse.
The Western countries still hold the major cards and
will not cede power either willingly or gladly. Indeed, opposition to the New International Information
Order continues. A conference at Talloires, France in
April 1981 of independent news media pilloried the
idea on the familiar grounds of press freedom. And

even though the United Nations General Assembly in December 1981 agreed to support the new order, Western financial support for the International Program for Developing Countries (IPDC) was not as vigorous as might have been expected. At the IPDC 35-nation Governing Council in Acapulco, Mexico in January 1982, there was much concern about methods of funding and control of funds.

In fact, funding mechanisms in UNESCO are part of the reason for the U.S. decision to leave the agency on January 1, 1985 and threats by 24 other industrial countries, including Britain, to do likewise. They are unwilling to put up with policies or actions which they consider against their national interests. Among these are the economic and information orders; what they see as a conspiracy between the Third World and the Soviet Union; a vast, unmanageable bureaucracy not amenable to their interests; and a loss of influence in decision-making. They put out a document, "The Crisis in UNESCO," suggesting that the organization consider a voting structure like the one used by the United Nations Industrial Development Organization (UNIDO). Under this voting arrangement major contributors have a veto over the allotment of funds.

But the politicization of the world will exist whether the U.S. remains in UNESCO or leaves. The U.S. National Commission for UNESCO recommended that the Federal Government should become more actively involved in UNESCO's work at all levels: appoint highly qualified delegates, and bring U.S. management techniques to help control the vast bureaucracy. Gains will be substantial: direct influence in the objectives of an organization it helped found--the words of Archibald MacLeish adorn its tribunals: "Since wars are made in the minds of men, it is in the minds of men that peace must be constructed"--and increased satisfaction in influencing and sharing. Lest this appear philosophical, it is well to recall that benefits from membership have already accrued: participation in the World Climate Research Program, which is supported by the International Oceanographic Commission of UNESCO, and the Scientific Committee on Oceanic Research; participation in the International Geological Correlation Program.

Internationalism is an ideal operating less on the basis of mutual interests and sharing of responsibilities for the distribution of world resources,

than on the definition of those responsibilities by the
rich few. The more the Third World presses its case,
however justified that case may be, the more it is likely to come up against a Western phalanx; at times that
phalanx might yield at weak points, but only to regroup
in others. But it will not compromise in areas of substance. And this is the apparent danger: that the
future of internationalism might be jeopardized by continued bickering; and the West, its back to the wall,
will decline further participation in international
tribunals, and leave the field to the Third World and
the Soviet Union. The resulting shift in world balance of power and the accompanying possibilities is
the real danger. The worse thing that can happen is
for the West to panic and leave the international
field. By remaining within these organizations and
supporting them under stressful condition, they will
establish a credibility, which has been much lacking
in the immediate past. And that might be worth saving
after the cut and thrust of the debate has ended.

Notes

1/ UNESCO. "The concept of a new international information order initiated among the non-aligned countries." UNESCO. Paris, 1976.

2/ UNESCO. Interim Report of the International Commission for the Study of Communication Problems. UNESCO. Paris, 1979, p. 19.

3/ UNESCO. Op. cit., 1976, p. 3.

4/ Desmond, R. W. The Information Process: World News Reporting to the Twentieth Century. Iowa City, Iowa: University of Iowa Press, 1978.

5/ Rogers, E. M. Modernization among Peasants: The Impact of Communication. New York: Holt, Rinehart & Winston, 1969. This author's more recent publication is a criticism of the trend of research in the sixties and the overemphasis of the role of communication in national development. Read, "Where we are in understanding the diffusion of innovations." Paper presented at the East-West Communication Institute Conference on Communication and Change: Ten Years After, Honolulu, 1975.

6/ Read, W. "Information as a National Resource." Journal of Communication. Winter 1979. Vol. 29, No. 1, p. 175.

7/ Oettinger, A. Quoted in Read, op. cit., 1979.

8/ UNESCO. Op. cit., 1976, p. 13.

9/ UNESCO. Op. cit., 1976, p. 13.

10/ Kroloff, G. and Cohen, S. "The New World Information Order." Report to the U.S. Senate Committee on Foreign Relations, Washington, D.C., Nov. 1977, cited in Journal of Communication by Read, op. cit., 1979, p. 177.

11/ UNESCO. Op. cit., 1979.

12/ Masmoudi, M. "The New International Information Order," document prepared for the International

Commission for the Study of Communication Problems.
UNESCO. Paris, 1978.

13/ Masmoudi, M. Op. cit., 1979.

14/ Tunstall, J. Op. cit., 1977.

15/ Masmoudi, M. Op. cit., 1978.

16/ Ibid., 1978.

17/ The New African, June 1979, p. 145.

18/ Masmoudi, M. Op. cit., 1978.

19/ Reshaping the International Order. Report
to the Club of Rome. New York: E. P. Dutton & Co.,
Inc., 1976, pp. 15-16.

20/ Lewis, A. The Evolution of the International
Economic Order. Princeton, N.J.: Princeton University
Press, 1978.

21/ Reshaping the International Order. Op. cit.,
1976, p. 19.

22/ Somavia, J. "Third World Participation in
International Communications, Perspectives after
Nairobi. Conceptual Considerations and Practical Pro-
posals." Paper delivered at the Seminar on Interna-
tional Communications and Third World Participation.
Amsterdam, Holland, September 1977, p. 14.

23/ Reshaping the International Order. Op. cit.,
1976, p. iii.

24/ Singham, A. "The Non-Aligned Movement."
United Nations Institute for Training and Research
News. Vol. xii, Spring 1980, p. 33.

25/ Splichal, S. & Ferligoj, A. "Balancing the
One-Way Flow of News in the World: The Case of Tanjug."
Ljubljani, University of Ljubljani, 1978.

26/ Splichal, S. & Ferligoj, A. Op. cit., 1978.

27/ Pinch, E. T. "The Third World and the
Fourth Estate: A Look at the Non-Aligned News Agencies Pool." U.S. Department of State, 1976-77.

28/ Sussman, L. Mass News Media and the Third World Challenge. Beverly Hills, Calif.: Sage Press, 1977.

29/ Gans, H. Discovering What's News. New York: Pantheon, 1979.

30/ Righter, R. Whose News? Politics, the Press and the Third World. New York: Times Books, 1978.

31/ Gans. Op. cit., 1979.

32/ Matta, Fernando, R. "The Latin American Concept of News." Journal of Communication. Vol. 29, No. 2, Spring 1979.

33/ McNelly, J. T. "International News for Latin America." Journal of Communication. Vol. 29, No. 2, Spring 1979.

34/ Pasquali, Antonio. "Latin America: Our Image or Theirs?" In UNESCO, Getting the Message Across. Paris: UNESCO, 1975.

35/ Gerbner, G. & G. Marvanyi. "The Many Worlds of the World's Press," Journal of Communication 28(1), Winter 1977.

36/ Martin, Richard R., J. McNelly, F. Izcaray. "Is Media Exposure Unidimensional? A Socioeconomic Approach." Journalism Quarterly 53, Winter 1976, pp. 619-625.

37/ Howkins, John. "What is the World Administrative Radio Conference." Journal of Communication, Vol. 29, No. 1, Winter 1979.

38/ The Yaounde Declaration, Adopted by the Intergovernmental Conference on Communication Policies in Africa, July 1980.

39/ UNESCO. Intergovernmental Conference on Communication Policies in Africa. Speech delivered by Secretary-General, Amadou-Mahtar M'Bow at Yaounde Cameroun and published in Belgrade, Yugoslavia, October 1980, p. 34.

40/ The idea previously came up at the Intergovernmental Conference at Kuala Lumpur in 1979 and discussed at the Intergovernmental Council of the

Non-Aligned Countries for the Coordination of Information at Lome, Togo, April 1979 and Baghdad, June 1980.

41/ UNESCO. Op. cit., 1980, p. 12.

42/ UNESCO. Interim Report of the International Commission for the Study of Communication Policies. UNESCO. Paris, 1978, p. 23.

43/ Ibid., pp. 15-18.

44/ Ibid., p. 15.

45/ Ibid., p. 24.

46/ Robin Chandler Duke, the chief U.S. delegate to the meeting of UNESCO's 21st General Conference in the New York Times, 2/15/81.

47/ This was placed in sharp perspective by Frank Campbell, the Minister of Information of the Republic of Guyana...We want a situation in which your journalists would come to our countries, understand our reality and not simply say that if we don't run our affairs the same way as you run yours, then we are backward or a dictatorship...Look at it another way. A journalist from Guyana wanting to go to the U.S. has to comply with normal visa requirements. Very often he is refused. But if we refuse a visa to a U.S. journalist, then it's a press freedom matter. Let's have universality...The New York Times, 2/15/81.

Appendix I

Iran's confrontation with the U.S. illustrates many of the points raised. The authors discuss the religious bias in reporting Iran.

Religion is one of the major cultural barriers for American reporters covering Iran (and for their editors back home). In the present context, moreover, it has emerged as the most difficult one for journalists to breach...

...For the Western journalist, non-Christian clergy and religious practices are "other." Ceremonies, beliefs, clerical conduct, and the relationship of religion to society as a whole are judged by Western standards, and the inevitable consequence is misinterpretation and distortion. (p. 32)

...The news media's emphasis on what they have taken to be the religious and traditionalist sources of the struggle builds on the inbred suspicion of Americans towards non-Christian cultures as being somehow primitive, riddled with superstition, and most importantly, reactionary-- a roadblock in the way of progress. (p. 31)

Such comments are not isolated. They belong only to the sensitive, too few of whom adorn any administration's portals. In a letter to the New York Times, anthropology professor, Mary Bateson, former dean of social sciences and humanities at the University of Northern Iran, and daughter of Margaret Mead, wrote:

"It is correct to attribute the original failure of United States intelligence in Iran to self-reinforcing wishful thinking, but the U.S. continued to be inept long after the widespread opposition to the Shah had become clear. U.S. attitudes towards Iran have suffered a second distortion, and that distortion is rooted in our apparent inability to understand religious movements.

197

"Although many aspects of the political outcome are still unclear, the revolution in Iran is a religious movement, comparable to the civil rights movement or the Ghandian movement. It involves thousands of people who are not especially pious, and it is fueled even among the secular classes by a longing for integrity which is far from fanaticism.

"For the U.S. Government the Iranian revolution represents a political and economic setback, but for the Iranian people, Islamic government represents a model of justice and truth and a rejection of corruption and opportunism.

"The fundamentally religious base of the movement can be seen in a kind of joyfulness, in a willingness to sacrifice life, comfort and economic advantage, and in the essentially disciplined and nonviolent behavior of the crowds (remarkably few persons have so far been attacked by the people). Above all, it can be seen in the use of a rhetoric traditional in Shiism and frightening to those who do not share in it. Imam Khomeini has been consistently misrepresented by the American media because of a failure of understanding.

"This failure is all the more frightening since we can expect it to be repeated unless we undertake a fundamental reappraisal of the role of religion in the world today. We are in the midst of a reassurance in Islam that is affecting country after country and will be one of the principal factors in world affairs in the years to come.

"U.S. policy makers, who collate information country by country and think primarily in geopolitical terms, seem unable to think in terms of any international ideological movement except Communism. Thus, in addition to an Iran desk or a Pakistan desk in the State Department, there is an urgent need of mechanisms for

thinking about the great transnational
religions.

"Such an effort must be scholarly and
sympathetic; it must transcend the
fashionable tendency to see religion
either as fanaticism or as a cloak for
other interests; it must be premised
on a recognition that for vast numbers
of the world's people the symbols of
religion sum up their highest aspirations."

The New York Times
February 20, 1979

Appendix II

Letter to the New York Times, 11/23/78
Guyana: Fact and the Interpretation of Fact

The mass suicide in Guyana provides an excellent point of reference for considering facts and the interpretation of facts in a free press and in a controlled press; and also, the flow of news between rich countries and poor countries--the so-called Third World. Indeed, elements of the Guyana situation are precisely those UNESCO has been discussing at its November meeting.

Third World countries are disturbed at the continuing monopoly of news and news sources by rich nations and also by the power of these nations to interpret and to decide on issues quite beyond their own power to respond. This is called news imbalance. Briefly, the rich nations have the media and the power which goes with it. The Third World does not have either the vast resources of media, nor the media coverage and their voices are correspondingly muted. Also, lack of manpower, technology and pressing national priorities stand in the way of media development. Unable to compete on equal terms, they are unable to fashion adequate responses for themselves and are therefore prey to the larger more sophisticated media resources of rich nations. It is a highly sensitive issue, involving not only news and news media, but economics and politics, for it is only too apparent that control of news media is associated with moneyed interests, which are heavily political.

Western countries have a philosophical creed which forms the basis of the practice of journalism and media in general: litertarianism from which the basic tenets of a free press derives. Freedom of information is the doctrine which, like the holy sacrament, inspires worship among its adherents. The Communists, on the other hand, make no such boast. News and its dissemination is subject to the interests and ideology of the Communist party. News is ideological and there is little pretense about it. News is interpreted according to the dictates of party dogma and the extent to which it furthers the objectives of the party.

But on occasion Western newspapers can equal the
Communists in the interpretation of a news event, particularly as it concerns the Third World. Here all
the cliches apply. The reporter, constrained by facts,
deadline, and a watchful city editor, is allowed full
use of his dramatic possibilities. Sensation replaces
sobriety, and responsibility in reporting a story is
defined more in terms of what metropolitan readers expect rather than demands of integrity, enquiry and objectivity. The generalization takes over; personal
beliefs and attitudes become as important as facts;
the word of a wayward traveller becomes gospel; gossip
at a local bar is an attributable source. Metropolitan reporters who would not dream of reporting a story
without checking all the angles now do so without scru-
ple. In reporting Europe, generally, an understandable
caution circumscribes most copy. In reporting the
Third World everything becomes grist for the mill and
catastrophes, disasters and coups d'etat are an admixture of fact and interpretation, integrated with casual
concern. Most important, however, are the psychological elements in the story which reveal deep bias.

Look, for instance, at the New York Times edition,
Monday, November 20th, describing the state of affairs
in Guyana:

"The violence on the streets of the capital
is the most tangible evidence to outsiders
of the chaotic condition of the country
since it gained independence from Britain
12 years ago."

Chaos is associated with political independence, with
the accompanying, though unspoken, inference that
Guyana cannot govern itself. The reporter did not consider that colonialism manufactured its own chaos.
Furthermore, violence does not need any specific context in which to make its unfortunate presence felt.
Many factors spawn violence and politics may be one
among others, such as injustice and oppression, factors more associated with the metropolitan aspects of
it. The sentence creates images with all the negative
assumptions which that implies: inferiority and tur-
moil.

Quoting from the same article: "The language
is mostly pidgin English." This is not true in
Guyana where English is spoken by a majority of the

202

inhabitants, who indeed, know no other language. The phrase "Pidgin English" tries to describe and, perhaps, explain the use of language which is heavily accented and figurative, but it succeeds in conjuring up only the pejorative. I have myself tried to explain and to understand the rich varieties in language structure and from existing between the South and the North of the United States, but it would be idle to refer to this diversity as "pidgin English."

Finally, to quote from the same article:

"The present reality of Guyana is probably most accurately reflected in its slums, with their dilapidated, two-story wooden frame houses that share outdoor water faucets and outhouses."

The bias here is clear. Poverty is by no means new to the Third World, but the efforts to end it, deserve commendation. Missing is mention of the new housing units which surround the capital of the country. The negative aspects of Guyana are singled out for special attention because it is these which convey the help-lessness, which is part of the psychological dependence, which rich nations like to see persist, which provides them with justification for their own courses of action and allows them to feel superior.

Slums are not new to most cities and the Third World does not have a monopoly on them, but it would be a mistake to believe that they reflect anything but the material conditions of peoples' lives. The will to fight the enormous conditions of poverty and development is surely the present reality in most Third World countries. The reporter errs when he does not see this and is incapable of understanding the move-ment towards change and self-sufficiency. He reports from the vantage point of privilege and material well-being. Sadly, many more believe him than ought to and this is one of the main criticisms from the Third World.

Of equal concern is the use of language to sup-port the national psyche and conceal truths too dif-ficult to recognize. Thus, various euphemisms describe urban decay: "run-down neighborhoods," "homes of the underprivileged," "economically depressed areas." But "slums" belong to the Third World.

203

Ten years ago Ronald Segal wrote in the <u>Race</u> <u>War</u> about the arrogance of racial superiority and biased reporting during the Belgian paratroop invasion of Zaire to free its nationals. The protests from Africa could scarcely be heard above the din of Belgian justification for an unwarranted action. The situations of course differ, but they both reveal a painful truth and that is the vulnerability of those nations which do not have powerful voices in the marketplace.

Guyana will be known more by the tragic occurrence at Jonestown than a place where disillusioned American citizens, alienated from their own society, sought peace in a multi-racial environment. One looked in vain for mention of Guyana's hospitality in allowing them to seek a place of refuge.

Appendix III

Reply of The New York Times

The New York Times
229 West 43 Street
New York, N.Y. 10026

Charlotte Curtis
Associate Editor

December 1, 1978

Dear Mr. Gibbons,

Your article is an interesting one, but we
are faced with a severe space problem and there's
just no way we can accommodate it. I'm so sorry,
and thanks very much for thinking of the Op-Ed
page.

Sincerely,

(Sgd.) Charlotte Curtis

/kh
Enclosure

R. Arnold Gibbons
Assistant Professor of Communications &
Director, Inter-American Affairs
Hunter College
695 Park Avenue
New York, N.Y. 10021

Appendix IV

The case of the U.S. vs. Frank W. Snepp iii and the significance it has for the First Amendment is instructive. Snepp, a former employee of the CIA wrote a book, Decent Interval, about the activities of his employer in the final days of Vietnam. The CIA, while acknowledging that the book contained no classified information, took him to court.

According to the CIA, Snepp broke a contract which required him to submit to them all writings concerning the CIA for pre-publication review. This is in itself a gross violation of First Amendment rights, but the Court held that a man can sign away his rights. But the Court went beyond this. It held that all government employees, newspaper and magazine publishers, indeed, anyone exposed to confidential sources, even in the absence of a contract, such as the one Snepp was under, can be so restricted. Both present and former employees involved in more than 30 government agencies, which can classify documents are subject to the ruling.

The implications of this decision for the press is clear. If Snepp, or anyone else for that matter, exposed to confidential information, writes a book and publishes it, without first submitting it to the agency he worked for, the publisher is liable for contempt of court and be sent to jail.

According to Robert Berstein, president of Random House, "they have set up a censorship system. There are no rules of any kind. They have said that an organization that is criticized can censor its critic."

"...I am appalled, Professor Thomas Emerson of Yale said. "If one thing is clear, it is that for a Government to impose that kind of blanket inhibition on its employees is a kind of action that is simply not governed by normal contract rules. It raises First Amendment rules about the right of an employee, and the right of the public to obtain information and the right of the press to publish it."

207

And Alan Dershowitz, Harvard Law School professor, specializing in First Amendment cases said:

> "...It's a loaded gun...it contains extra-
> ordinarily open and loose language...it's
> the greatest example of overreaching and
> lack of judicial restraint in our memory.
> None of us can think of any other example
> where the Government asked for a remedy
> and the Court gave so much more..." (The
> New York Times, March 11, 1980).

Henry Kaufman of the Association of American Publishers said: "the court's opinion provides the
theoretical underpinnings for a significant expansion
of government secrecy at all levels." And Nat Hentoff,
a vigorous defender of First Amendment Rights, declared: "In drastic essence, the High Court has
usurped the law-making powers of Congress and has gone
a long way towards enacting an American version of
the British Official Secrets Act." (Cited in the
Village Voice, March 31, 1980.)

In Britain, the Official Secrets Act is but one
of the restrictions placed on journalists, which include the "D" Notices (request to journalists not to
publish material in the interests of national security); laws of libel and laws of obscenity; rules governing contempt of court and parliamentary privilege,
which have all but restrained the practicing journalist from performing his work. "The result is that
Britain has acquired in this century an increasingly
secret form of government about which the Press is
able to do very little without infringing the provisions of the Official Secrets Act." 1/

Also, the erosion of the power of the press by
government legislation has coincided with the crisis
in press legitimacy. Basically, the economic realities of the British press, which has increasingly
come to be subjected to monopoly ownership and multinational corporations, is at odds with the traditional nineteenth century view of press freedom. In
what sense is a press largely owned by seven multinational corporations free? If such a press is free
then whose freedom is it? The debate over freedom
of the press and the lack of it in Britain, is compounded by the confusion and inability of successive
Royal Commissions on the Press (1949, 1962, 1977)

208

to do anything substantive about the crisis despite
exhaustive recommendations. But what they have done
is "to try to rehabilitate the press in two ways--
by promoting, modifying and updating the liberal
theory of a free press in a way that takes into account changes in its ownership and structure. 2/

At the same time they tended to ignore the other
convincing evidence of the structure of the press,
which still relies on, encourages and feeds on class
interests, 3/ depends on institutional sources for
news, 4/ and is in general unfair to the trade
unions. 5/ What the Commissions did not realize (or
they realized but would not, or could not admit because it was itself a part of the elitism, which go-
verns English society), was that the nineteenth century idealism of press freedom had radically changed
and that this change was one which the society could
not tolerate since it was at odds with notions of
democracy in which it had steadfastly believed. A
great deal of hypocrisy underwrites current attitudes
to the press in a country in which the only newspaper
with no commercial interests outside of publishing,
is the Daily Worker, a Communist newspaper.

Snepp was not the only case which imperiled the
First Amendment rights; rather, it was one in a
series of assaults. Notable is that of Gannet vs.
DePasqualte, where the Court ruled that judges could
close pretrial hearings to the press and to the public. Also, the decision in Herbert vs. Lando, in
which the Supreme Court held that a public figure,
suing for libel could ask questions in the pretrial
about the thoughts and opinions of reporters while
they were preparing the material.

The net result of this series of decisions has
been to effectively dampen the vigor with which
journalists traditionally operate and to supress the
ardor that sometimes accompany their professional
pursuit. In addition, the narrow focus of the law
defined by the Supreme Court, has tended to encourage
public figures to sue for libel, a consequence of
which is an increase in legal fees. But the narrow
interpretation of law and the assault by the combined justices on the First Amendment has markedly
affected newsroom practices.

"...practices, which would have been unheard of a few years ago, include formal

procedures for destroying notes or transferring them to an officer of the news
organization; the issuance of wallet-sized
cards to reporters with statements to be
read aloud in court stating the news organization's objection in the event a judge
bars the press from the courtroom, and
editors' compiling detailed memorandums in
the course of an investigation that would
indicate in any future libel suit that the
reporter was trying to produce a fair
story and not trying to defame the person
being investigated." (The New York Times,
April 7, 1980)

The Declaration of Fundamental Principles
Concerning the Contribution of the Mass
Media to Strengthening Peace and Interna-
tional Understanding, the Promotion of
Human Rights and to Countering Racialism,
Apartheid and Incitement to War

Adopted on November 22, 1978 by
the UNESCO General Conference

Article I

The strengthening of peace and international
understanding, the promotion of human rights and the
countering of racialism, apartheid and incitement to
war demand a free flow and wider and better balanced
dissemination of information. To this end, the mass
media have a leading contribution to make. This
contribution will be the more effective to the extent
that the information reflects the different aspects
of the subject dealt with.

Article II

1. The exercise of freedom of opinion, expression and information, recognized as an integral part
of human rights and fundamental freedoms, is a vital
factor in the strengthening of peace and international understanding.

2. Access by the public to information should
be guaranteed by the diversity of the sources and
means of information available to it, thus enabling
each individual to check the accuracy of facts and to
appraise events objectively. To this end, journalists
must have freedom to report and the fullest possible
facilities of access to information. Similarly, it is
important that the mass media be responsible to concerns of peoples and individuals, thus promoting the
participation of the public in the elaboration of information.

3. With a view to the strengthening of peace and
international understanding, to promoting human rights
and to countering racialism, apartheid and incitement

to war, the mass media throughout the world, by reason
of their role, contribute effectively to promoting
human rights in particular by giving expression to oppressed peoples who struggle against colonialism, neo-
colonialism, foreign occupation and all forms of racial
discrimination and oppression and who are unable to
make their voices heard within their own territories.

4. If the mass media are to be in a position to
promote the principles of this declaration in their
activities, it is essential that journalists and other
agents of the mass media, in their own country or
abroad, be assured of protection guaranteeing them the
best conditions for the exercise of their profession.

Article III

1. The mass media have an important contribution
to make to the strengthening of peace and international understanding and in countering racialism, apartheid
and incitement to war.

2. In countering aggressive war, racialism,
apartheid and other violations of human rights which
are _inter_ _alia_ spawned by prejudice and ignorance, the
mass media by disseminating information on the aims,
aspirations, cultures and needs of all people, contribute to eliminate ignorance and misunderstanding
between peoples, to make nationals of a country sensitive to the needs and desires of others, to ensure
the respect of the rights and dignity of all nations,
all peoples and all individuals without distinction
of race, sex, language, religion or nationality and
to draw attention to the great evils which afflict
humanity, such as poverty, malnutrition and diseases,
thereby promoting the formulation by states of policies best able to promote the reduction of international tension and the peaceful and the equitable
settlement of international disputes.

Article IV

The mass media have an essential part to play in
the education of young people in a spirit of peace,
justice, freedom, mutual respect and understanding,
in order to promote human rights, equality of rights
as between all human beings and all nations, and economic and social progress. Equally they have an important role to play in making known the views and
aspirations of the younger generation.

212

Article V

In order to respect freedom of opinion, expression and information and in order that information may reflect all points of view, it is important that the points of view presented by those who consider that the information published or disseminated about them has seriously prejudiced their effort to strengthen peace and international understanding, to promote human rights or to counter racialism, apartheid and incitement to war be disseminated.

Article VI

For the establishment of a new equilibrium and greater reciprocity in the flow of information, which will be conducive to the institution of a just and lasting peace and to the economic and political independence of the developing countries, it is necessary to correct the inequalities in the flow of information to and from developing countries, and between those countries. To this end, it is essential that their mass media should have conditions and resources enabling them to gain strength and expand, and to cooperate both among themselves and with the mass media in developed countries.

Article VII

By disseminating more widely all of the information concerning the objectives and principles universally accepted which are the bases of the resolutions adopted by the different organs of the United Nations, the mass media contribute effectively to the strengthening of peace and international understanding, to the promotion of human rights, as well as to the establishment of a more just and equitable international economic order.

Article VIII

Professional organizations, and people who participate in the professional training of journalists and other agents of the mass media and who assist them in performing their functions in a responsible manner should attach special importance to the principles of this declaration when drawing up and ensuring application of their codes of ethics.

Article IX

In the spirit of this declaration, it is for the international community to contribute to the creation of the conditions for a free flow and wider and more balanced dissemination of information, and the conditions for the protection, in the exercise of their functions, of journalists and other agents of the mass media. UNESCO is well placed to make a valuable contribution in this respect.

Article X

1. With due respect for constitutional provisions designed to guarantee freedom of information and for the applicable international instruments and agreements, it is indispensable to create and maintain throughout the world the conditions which make it possible for the organizations and persons professionally involved in the dissemination of information to achieve the objectives of this declaration.

2. It is important that a free flow and wider and better balanced dissemination of information be encouraged.

3. To this end, it is necessary that states should facilitate the procurement, by the mass media in the developing countries, of adequate conditions and resources enabling them to gain strength and expand, and that they should support cooperation by the latter both among themselves and with the mass media in developed countries.

4. Similarly, on a basis of equality of rights mutual advantage, and respect for the diversity of cultures which go to make up the common heritage of mankind, it is essential that bilateral and multilateral exchanges of information among all states, and in particular between those which have different economic and social systems be encouraged and developed.

Article XI

For this declaration to be fully effective it is necessary, with due respect for the legislative and administrative provisions and the other obligation of member states, to guarantee the existence of favorable conditions for the operation of the mass media, in conformity with the provisions of the Universal Declaration of Human Rights and with the corresponding principles proclaimed in the International Covenant on Civil and Political Rights adopted by the General Assembly of the United Nations in 1966.

oOo

Index

Universal Declaration of
  Human Rights, 14, 18
United Press Internation-
  al (UPI), 16, 71, 144

Vietnam, 56, 73, 78
Voice of Germany, 127

West Germany, 31
Western countries, 8, 15;
  position with regard to
  free flow of information,
  42, 53, 55, 73, 104, 125

Winks, Roger, 67
World Administrative Radio
  Conference, 183
World War II, 24
World System, 49

Yaounde Declaration, 185
Yugoslavia, 164

Zaire, 94, 171
Zambia, 26
Zimbabwe, 7

ABOUT THE AUTHOR

Arnold Gibbons, Associate Professor of Communications at Hunter College of the City University of New York, and a former Director of its Inter-American Studies Program, studied philosophy at the University of London. He has graduate degrees in communications and educational technology from Cornell and Syracuse Universities.

Dr. Gibbons has worked both at the British Broadcasting Corporation (BBC), London and as an editor at the Deutsche Welle, the Voice of Germany, Koln, West Germany. He is the author of the recently published monograph <u>Namibia: the Legal Issues</u> for the United Nations and has published many articles in journals and books dealing with communications and development.